# Poptropica® English

## STUDENT BOOK 3

## Space Island

T0385793

Aaron Jolly • Viv Lambert
**Series advisor:** David Nunan

**Pearson Education Limited**
Edinburgh Gate
Harlow
Essex CM20 2JE
England
and Associated Companies throughout the world.

Poptropica English

© Pearson Education Limited 2015

**Based on the work of Viv Lambert**

**The rights of Aaron Jolly and Viv Lambert to be identified as authors of this work have been asserted by them in accordance with the Copyright, Designs and Patents Act 1988.**

**Stories on pages 16, 26, 38, 48, 60, 70, 82, and 92 by Catherine Prentice. The rights of Catherine Prentice to be identified as author of this work have been asserted by her in accordance with the Copyright, Designs and Patents Act 1988.**

**Phonics syllabus and activities by Rachel Wilson**

Editorial and project management by hyphen

All rights reserved; no part of this publication may be reproduced, stored in a retrieval system, or transmitted in any form or by any means, electronic, mechanical, photocopying, recording, or otherwise without the prior written permission of the Publishers.

First published 2015

Twelfth impression 2019

ISBN: 978-1-292-09103-7

Set in Fiendstar 15/24pt

Printed in Slovakia by Neografia

**Illustrators:** Humberto Blanco (Sylvie Poggio Artists Agency), Anja Boretzki (Good Illustration), Chan Cho Fai, Chiara Buccheri (Lemonade Illustration), Scott Burroughs (Deborah Wolfe Ltd), Lee Cosgrove, Leo Cultura, Bill Greenhead (Illustration), Marek Jagucki, Daniel Limon (Beehive Illustration), Mark Ruffle (The Organisation), Anjan Sarkar (Good Illustration) and Dickie Seto

**Picture Credits:** The Publishers would like to thank the following for their kind permission to reproduce their photographs: (Key: b-bottom; c-center; l-left; r-right; t-top)
(Key: b-bottom; c-centre; l-left; r-right; t-top)
**123RF.com:** 85r, akulamatiau 85l, antonel 14 (g), petar dojkic 47t, Eric Isselee 58/3, Jose Manuel Gelpi Diaz 35l, Olga Kovalenko 62 (a), Roger McClean 95tl, Konstantin Shaklein 102r, Eric Simard 82 (c), Thawat Tanhai 14 (a), tobkatrina 98 (b), Marco Tomasini 30r; **Alamy Images:** amana images inc. 23l, Cultura Creative (RF) 115 (a), dbimages 94br, Danita Delimont 22b, Glowimages RM 71l, Sally and Richard Greenhill 70r, Juniors Bildarchiv GmbH 47c, NASA Photo 87, Simon Reddy 95tr, Sinibomb Images 66/5, Tetra Images 66/1, Rob Walls 66/2; **Fotolia.com:** 2happy 14 (f), 3532studio 95br, A_Lein 78/17 (8), Denis Aglichev 62 (g), ahavelaar 98 (c), andreiuc88 14 (h), 20 (g rainbow), Anterovium 14 (c), 20 (e ants), 20 (f), aquariagirl1970 62 (c), 74 (d), Azaliya (Elya Vatel) 38 (e), baibaz 92/7, Beauty ofLife 62 (h), bergamont 20 (b), bst2012 94tl, Jacek Chabraszewski 104, chungking 62 (b), DenisNata 86 (a), Dhoxax 47b (spider), Dionisvera 92/5, dule964 20 (a), 20 (d birds), Jaimie Duplass 80 (basketball), emprise 58/2, epantha 20 (e spiders), Zakharov Evgeniy 62 (e), Fotofermer 78/17 (3), 89/8, Gamut Stock Images 98 (e), Gelpi 25r, Roman Gorielov 83l, Gresei 92/1, heinteh 50 (g), Václav Hroch 98 (d), humbak 32/3 (right), Eric Isselée 44 (f), jagodka 44 (g), julianwphoto 30l, karandaev 50 (b), 50 (h), ivan kmit 20 (d trees), 20 (g trees), 89/3, Yuriy Korchagin 75r, Vera Kuttelvaserova 44 (e), Lucky Dragon 98 (a), lurs 62 (f), Arlo Magicman 102l, mamahoohooba 46br, Marek 54 (tile), mariesacha 82 (a), marima-design 54 (stones), mates 92/2, mediagram 32/2 (right), melkerw 32/1, Nik Merkulov 50 (a), mettus 54 (glass), Monkey Business 71r, 115 (c), 115 (d), Mushy 78/17 (4), nata777_7 92/9, Natika 86 (f), 86 (h), 92/3, nipaporn 92/10, nito 32/2 (left), Duncan Noakes 75l, Sergey Novikov 83r, patboon 74 (h), pelegelkalay 50 (c), pongsak1 86 (d), paul prescott 54 (fish), rukanoga 50 (f), Gino Santa Maria 35r, 39r, Elena Schweitzer 32/3 (left), SergeyS 62 (d), shishiga 47b (duck), spline_x 94bl, StockPhotosArt 58/1, stocksolutions 89/5, TrudiDesign 89/2, underworld 14 (b), V.R.Murralinath 78/17 (1), valery121283 92/8, victorhabbick 74 (e), Malyshchyts Viktar 86 (g), volff 86 (e), wajan 74 (c), Jamie Wilson 30tr, xy 74 (j), zelenka68 50 (d), Artranq 115 (b); **Getty Images:** Michael & Patricia Fogden 30tc, Gusto Images 95tc, Jupiterimages 95bl, kate_sept2004 70l, Sri Maiava Rusden 46t; **Imagemore Co., Ltd:** 74 (i); **Imagestate Media:** John Foxx Collection 38 (f); **Pearson Education Ltd:** Studio 8 13l, 25l, Jon Barlow 11r, 13r, 80t, Gareth Boden 10, Trevor Clifford 11l, 27l, 27r, 37l, 37r, 49, 63l, 63r, 73l, 73r, 78/16 (1), 78/16 (2), 78/16 (3), 78/16 (4), 78/16 (5), 80tc, 80b, 80bc, 97l, 97r, 115bl; **PhotoDisc:** Alan D. Carey 38 (c); **Photolibrary.com:** Ryan McVay. Digital Vision 66/3; **Shutterstock. com:** Alex Avich 62 (i), AlexKalashnikov 46bl, Zaneta Baranowska 92/6, bikeriderlondon 22t, Stepan Bormotov 44 (c), Tony Campbell 44 (d), Donna Ellen Coleman 58br, Alexander Dashewsky 89/1, Denizo71 66/4, Digital Media Pro 78/17 (5), fivespots 38 (b), 38 (g), Gavran333 86 (b), Mark Higgins 30tl, Chris Hill 74 (b), Jiang Hongyan 38 (d), irin-k 14 (d), Eric Isselee 39l, Mariyana Misaleva 78/17 (6), Juriah Mosin 61r, 115br, Maks Narodenko 89/7, Nitr 89/6, PathDoc 58bl, paulaphoto 23r, 61l, photobank.ch 74 (a), Olga Polyakova 78/17 (7), Alex Staroseltsev 44 (a), Tracy Starr 47b (parrot), Aleksey Stemmer 38 (a), Winai Tepsuttinun 50 (e), Attl Tibor 82 (b), Mogens Trolle 44 (b), Analia Valeria Urani 94tr, Alla Ushakova 89/4, vbmark 78/17 (2), Lilyana Vynogradova 86 (c), Pan Xunbin 14 (e), 20 (h), Yellowj 92/4, Bershadsky Yuri 20 (c), Pierre-Yves Babelon 74 (g); **Sozaijiten:** 47b (iguana), 74 (f)

All other images © Pearson Education

Every effort has been made to trace the copyright holders and we apologize in advance for any unintentional omissions. We would be pleased to insert the appropriate acknowledgement in any subsequent edition of this publication.

# Contents

# Scope and sequence

## Welcome

| | |
|---|---|
| **Vocabulary:** | **Numbers:** twenty-one to fifty<br>**Days of the week:** Sunday, Monday, Tuesday, Wednesday, Thursday, Friday, Saturday<br>**Months of the year:** January, February, March, April, May, June, July, August, September, October, November, December |
| **Structures:** | What's your favorite day? My favorite day is Sunday.<br>When were you born? I was born in January.<br>Were you born in May? Yes, I was. / No, I wasn't. I was born in June. |

## 1  Nature

| | | |
|---|---|---|
| **Vocabulary:** | **Nature:** birds, sun, clouds, trees, animal, pond, mushrooms, rock, insects, flowers, butterflies, wind, ants, sky, worms, spiders, roses, rainbow | **Values:** Play outside. Play safe! |
| **Structures:** | How many animals are there? There's one purple animal.<br>How many birds are there? There are two blue birds.<br>There are some spiders. / There aren't any spiders.<br>Is there a rainbow? Yes, there is. / No, there isn't.<br>Is there any wind? Yes, there's some wind. / No, there isn't any wind.<br>Are there any ants? Yes, there are. / No, there aren't. | **Cross-curricular:**<br>**Math:** Plus, minus, equals<br><br>**Phonics:** air, ear<br>hair, year |

## 2  Me

| | | |
|---|---|---|
| **Vocabulary:** | **Physical characteristics:** blond hair, dark eyebrows, brown eyes, curly hair, gray hair, glasses, a black mustache, a short beard, blue eyes, red hair, black beard, white teeth, big chin, long eyelashes, pink lips, red nose, big mouth | **Values:** Have good habits. Keep clean and healthy. |
| **Structures:** | I have glasses.<br>I don't have glasses.<br>He has dark eyebrows.<br>She doesn't have dark eyebrows.<br>Do you have long eyelashes? Yes, I do. / No, I don't.<br>Does he/she have curly hair? Yes, he/she does. / No, he/she doesn't. | **Cross-curricular:**<br>**Science:** Wild animals<br><br>**Phonics:** ay, er<br>say, dinner |

## 3  Pets

| | | |
|---|---|---|
| **Vocabulary:** | **Animal body parts:** tail, beak, wings, feathers, claws, fins, paws, whiskers, skin, fur<br>**Animal characteristics:** soft fur, a hard shell, sharp claws<br>**Adjectives:** cute, scary, fast, slow | **Values:** Take care of your pet. |
| **Structures:** | What does it look like? It has a tail. It doesn't have wings.<br>What do they look like? They have whiskers. They don't have fins.<br>Do you have a dog? Yes, I do. It's cute. / No, I don't.<br>Does it have soft fur? Yes, it does. / No, it doesn't. | **Cross-curricular:**<br>**Science:** Animal life cycles<br><br>**Phonics:** ea, oi<br>tea, oil |

## 4  Home

| | | |
|---|---|---|
| **Vocabulary:** | **Furnishings:** picture, stove, sofa, shower, sink, mirror, trash can, TV, computer, plant, closet, window<br>**Prepositions:** next to, behind, above, below, in front of<br>**Household items:** toothbrush, towels, pots, blankets, comb, shelf, pans, plates | **Values:** Help at home. |
| **Structures:** | There's a plant in the living room.<br>There are two plants in the living room.<br>The plant is below the mirror. / It's below the mirror.<br>The plants are below the mirror. / They're below the mirror.<br>Is the computer in the bedroom? Yes, it is. / No, it isn't. It's in the living room.<br>Are the plates on the shelf? Yes, they are. / No, they aren't. They're in the sink. | **Cross-curricular:**<br>**Art:** Mosaics<br><br>**Phonics:** a_e, i_e, o_e<br>cake, time, home |

## ⑤ Clothes

| | | |
|---|---|---|
| **Vocabulary:** | **Clothing:** a baseball cap, a sweatsuit, a polo shirt, shirt, shorts, jeans, a belt, a uniform, a jacket, a sweatshirt, flip-flops, sneakers, sandals, beanie, hiking boots, scarf, tights, ski jacket, wool sweater<br>**Material/style:** plain, colorful, fancy | **Values:** Be polite.<br><br>**Cross-curricular:**<br>Social science:<br>Household chores<br><br>**Phonics:** sc, sk, sm, sn, sp, squ, st, sw<br>scarf, skate, smell, snip, spoon, squid, star, swim |
| **Structures:** | What are you wearing? I'm wearing a baseball cap/sandals.<br>What's he/she wearing? He's/She's wearing a baseball cap/sandals.<br>Are you wearing a baseball cap/sandals? Yes, I am. / No, I'm not.<br>Is he/she wearing a baseball cap/sandals? Yes, he/she is. / No, he/she isn't.<br>This is my favorite scarf.<br>These are my favorite tights.<br>I love my scarf/tights. | |

## ⑥ Sports

| | | |
|---|---|---|
| **Vocabulary:** | **Abilities:** do taekwondo, catch a ball, play tennis, run, play baseball, ride a bike, play basketball, play soccer<br>**Sports facilities:** gym, baseball field, basketball court, running track, stadium, ski slope, beach, swimming pool, tennis court, soccer field | **Values:** Be active.<br>Exercise every day.<br><br>**Cross-curricular:**<br>Health: Exercise<br><br>**Phonics:** bl, fl, gl, pl, sl<br>black, flag, glass, plate, sleep |
| **Structures:** | I/He/She can run and jump.<br>I/He/She can run, but I/he/she can't jump.<br>Can you/he/she play tennis? Yes, I/he/she can. / No, I/he/she can't.<br>I/He/She was at the gym.<br>I/He/She wasn't at the gym. I/He/She was at the baseball field. | |

## ⑦ Food

| | | |
|---|---|---|
| **Vocabulary:** | **Fruit/vegetables:** peas, mangoes, carrots, cucumbers, plums, oranges, peaches, potatoes, tomatoes, strawberries, beans, broccoli, lettuce, spinach, cabbage, pears, apricots, avocadoes, cherries | **Values:** Stay healthy. Eat more fruit and vegetables.<br><br>**Cross-curricular:**<br>Science: Healthy eating plate<br><br>**Phonics:** br, cr, dr, fr, gr, pr, str, tr<br>brown, crab, drop, frog, green, press, string, train |
| **Structures:** | Do you like peas? Yes, I do. / No, I don't.<br>Does he/she like peas? Yes, he/she does. / No, he/she doesn't.<br>Is there any broccoli? Yes, there is. / No, there isn't.<br>Are there any pears? Yes, there are. / No, there aren't. | |

## ⑧ Things we do

| | | |
|---|---|---|
| **Vocabulary:** | **Actions:** listening to music, walking, sleeping, reading, doing homework, drinking, eating, cleaning, dancing, playing the piano, playing the trumpet, playing the flute, playing the violin, singing<br>**Adverbs of manner:** quickly, quietly, terribly, loudly, slowly | **Values:** Learn new things.<br>Develop your talents.<br><br>**Cross-curricular:**<br>Science: Flying machines<br><br>**Phonics:** ft, mp, nd, nt, sk, sp, st<br>left, bump, wind, paint, ask, wisp, nest |
| **Structures:** | What are you doing? I'm sleeping.<br>What are they doing? They're sleeping.<br>What's he/she doing? He's/She's sleeping.<br>Are you singing? Yes, I am. / No, I'm not.<br>Is he/she singing? Yes, he/she is. / No, he/she isn't.<br>Is he/she singing quietly? Yes, he/she is. / No, he/she isn't. He's/She's singing loudly. | |

# Welcome

Can understand a story

Can understand a story

2 🎧 A:03  **Listen, check (✓), and say.**

3 🎧 A:04  **Listen and sing. Then find the tifftiff plant.**

Hey boys! Hey girls!
Come with us to Space Island.
Look up, down, here, there.
Look around everywhere.
Where's the tifftiff plant?
Come on, come on,
Let's find the tifftiff plant!

WELCOME TO SPACE ISLAND

Hello. I'm Captain Conrad.

I'm President Pop. Welcome to Space Island.

My name's Katy.

I'm Kim.

I'm PROD 1.

And I'm PROD 2! Hello!

Can identify characters in a story

**4** Listen and say. Then circle the characters' favorite numbers.

A:05

| 21 twenty-one | 22 twenty-two | 23 twenty-three | 24 twenty-four | 25 twenty-five |
|---|---|---|---|---|
| 26 twenty-six | 27 twenty-seven | 28 twenty-eight | 29 twenty-nine | 30 thirty |
| 31 thirty-one | 32 thirty-two | 33 thirty-three | 34 thirty-four | 35 thirty-five |
| 36 thirty-six | 37 thirty-seven | 38 thirty-eight | 39 thirty-nine | 40 forty |
| 41 forty-one | 42 forty-two | 43 forty-three | 44 forty-four | 45 forty-five |
| 46 forty-six | 47 forty-seven | 48 forty-eight | 49 forty-nine | 50 fifty |

  **5** Listen and circle.

A:06

1   ( twenty-six / twenty-seven / twenty-eight )

2   ( thirty-two / thirty-four / thirty-nine )

3   ( twenty-three / thirty-three / sixty-three )

4   ( twenty-seven / thirty-seven / forty-seven )

  **6** Write five numbers. Then ask and answer.

33?    No. Up. ↑    40?    No. Down. ↓    36?    Yes! My turn.

**7**  Sing.

| | |
|---|---|
| Sunday | |
| Monday | |
| Tuesday | |
| Wednesday | |
| Thursday | |
| Friday | |
| Saturday | |

Seven days in a week –
What's your favorite day?
Oh, that's easy. It's Tuesday!
My favorite day, my favorite day,
My favorite day is Tuesday.

Seven days in a week –
What's your favorite day?
Oh, that's easy. It's Sunday!
My favorite day, my favorite day,
My favorite day is Sunday.

 **LOOK!**

| What's your **favorite day**? | My **favorite day** is Sunday. |
|---|---|

**8**  Listen and circle.

**1**  Mark    My favorite day is
( Monday / Tuesday / Wednesday ).

**2** Tina    My favorite day is
( Thursday / Friday / Saturday ).

**3** Sam    My favorite day is
( Saturday / Sunday / Monday ).

What's your favorite day?

My favorite day
is Friday.

**9**  Check (✓). Then ask, answer, and check (✓).

| | Me | (Friend 1) | (Friend 2) | (Friend 3) |
|---|---|---|---|---|
| Sunday | | | | |
| Monday | | | | |
| Tuesday | | | | |
| Wednesday | | | | |
| Thursday | | | | |
| Friday | | | | |
| Saturday | | | | |

**10**  **Listen and say. Then listen and number.**

| January | | February | | March | | April | |
|---|---|---|---|---|---|---|---|
| May | | June | | July | | August | |
| September | | October | | November | | December | |

**11**  **Listen and circle.**

**1** He was born in
( January / February /
March / April ).

**LOOK!**

| **When** were you **born**? | I was **born** in January. |
|---|---|
| Were you **born** in May? | Yes, I was. |
| | No, I wasn't. I was born in June. |

wasn't = was not

**2** She was born in ( May / June / July / August ).

**3** They were born in ( September / October / November / December ).

**12**  **Check (✓). Then ask, answer, and check (✓).**

| | Me | (Friend 1) | (Friend 2) | (Friend 3) |
|---|---|---|---|---|
| January | | | | |
| February | | | | |
| March | | | | |
| April | | | | |
| May | | | | |
| June | | | | |
| July | | | | |
| August | | | | |
| September | | | | |
| October | | | | |
| November | | | | |
| December | | | | |

When were you born?

I was born in July.

# 1 Nature

sun    clouds

birds

**1** ⭐ What do you know?

**2** 🎧 A:14 Listen and find. What's missing?

animal

mushrooms    rock    pond    insects

**3** 🎧 A:15 Listen and number.    **4** 🎧 A:16 Listen and say.

a ☐    b ☐    c ☐    d ☐

f ☐    g ☐    h ☐    i ☐

Can identify common nature words

trees

flowers

e

j

 **Listen and chant.**

A:17 / A:18

There's a pond, a blue pond.
There's a rock, a brown rock.
There's an animal, a purple animal.

There are birds, blue birds.
There are insects, pink insects.
There are flowers, yellow flowers.

6  **Look at the scene. Count and say.**

A:19 **LOOK!**

| | |
|---|---|
| How many animals **are there**? | **There's** one purple animal. |
| How many birds **are there**? | **There are** two blue birds. |

7  **Play a memory game.**

How many brown rocks are there?

There's one brown rock.

## 8 Listen and number. Then say.

A:20

VOCABULARY

a 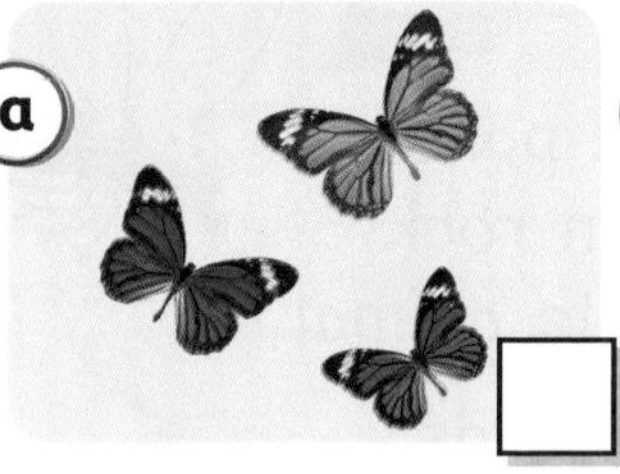

butterflies

b 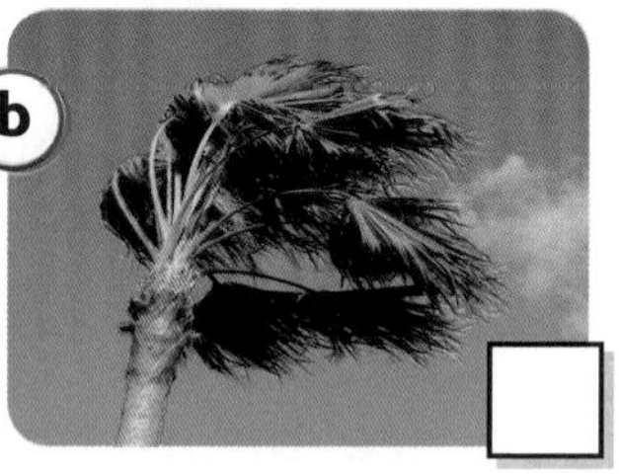

wind

c 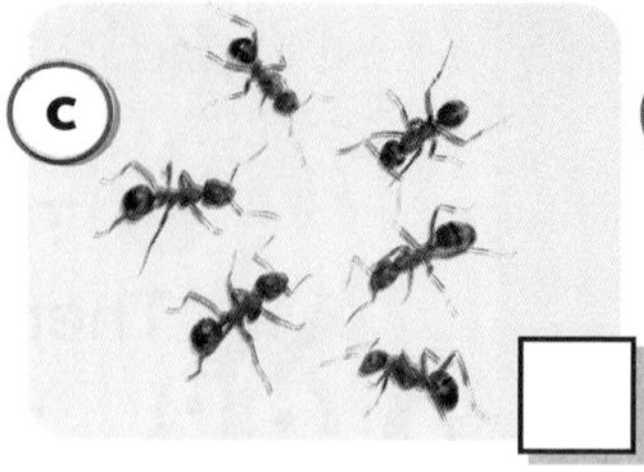

ants

d 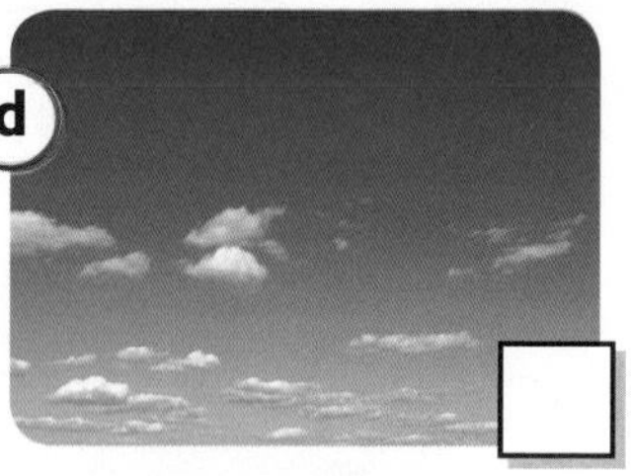

sky

e 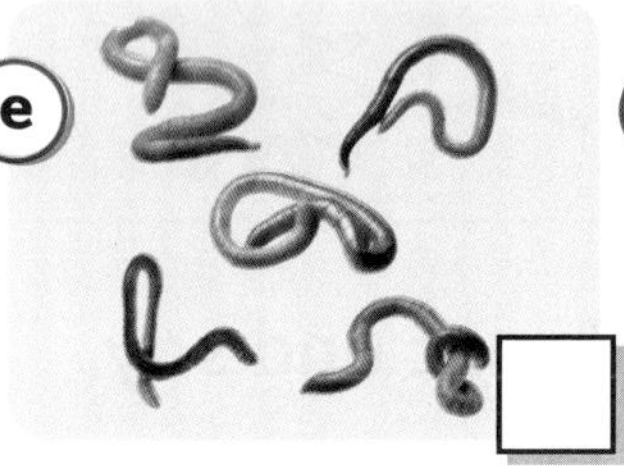

worms

f 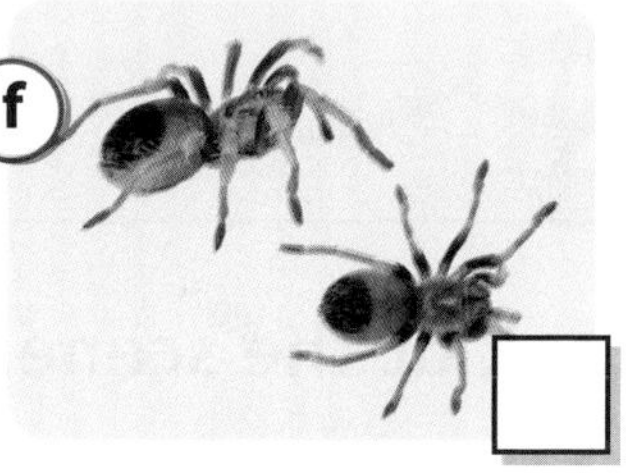

spiders

g 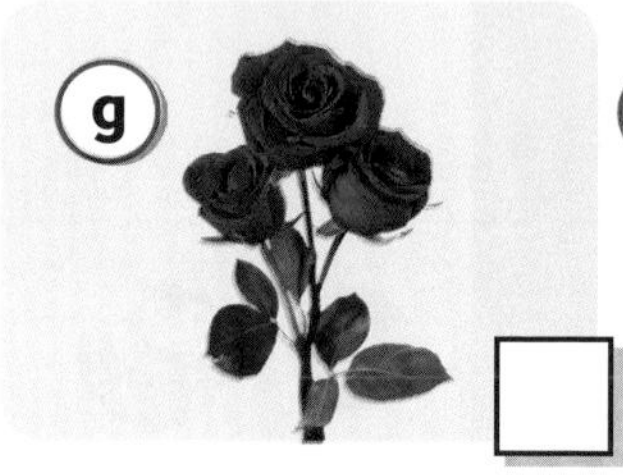

roses

h 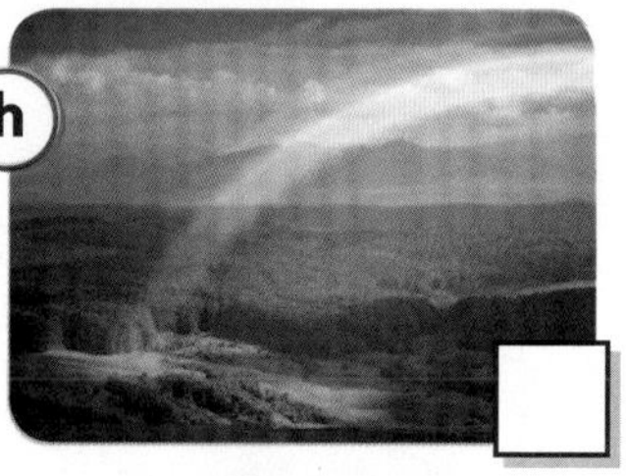

rainbow

## 9 Listen. Then sing and do the actions.

A:21 / A:22

SONG

How many birds are there?
There are seven birds.
There are six mushrooms.
There are five rocks.
Seven, six, five,
Stamp, stamp, stamp!

How many animals are there?
There are four animals.
There are three trees.
There are two clouds,
Four, three, two,
Clap, clap, clap!

How many ponds are there?
There's one pond.
One blue pond.
Only one blue pond,
Jump, jump, splash!

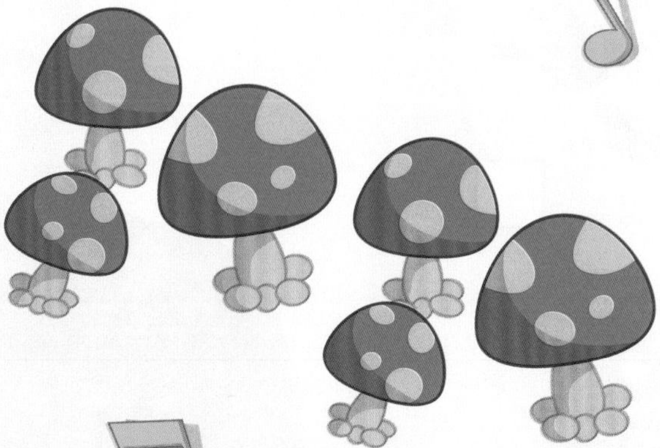



Can identify more nature words

## LOOK!

| There are **some** spiders. | There aren't **any** spiders. |
| --- | --- |
| Is there **a** rainbow? | Yes, there is. / No, there isn't. |
| Is there **any** wind? | Yes, there's **some** wind. / No, there isn't **any** wind. |
| Are there **any** ants? | Yes, there are. / No, there aren't. |

**10** A:24 **Listen and circle the correct screen. Then ask and answer.**

**11** **Look, ask, and answer.**

**SPEAKING**

1   At the library    2   At the park    3   At the museum    4   At the playground

There are some trees.

Yes, there are. Where are they?

Are there any children?

At the playground.

## LOOK!

| **Where** are they? | **At** the library. |
| --- | --- |
| **Where** is he? | **At** the museum. |

**1**
Is it big or small?
It's small.
What color is it?
It's orange.

**2**
Is this a tifftiff?
I don't know.

**3**
Aargh! It isn't a tifftiff!
It's an animal!

**4**
Oooh! Look, it's a tifftiff plant!
Ha, ha, ha!

**5**
Help! I'm in the pond!
Ha, ha, ha!

**6**
There aren't any tifftiffs here.
Hee, hee, hee!
It isn't funny!

13  **Role-play the story.**

Can understand a simple story / Can role-play a story

**14** **Look at the story. Read and write the number of the picture.**

**a**  PROD 1 isn't happy.  `6`

**b**  There are seven flowers.  ☐

**c**  There's a tifftiff plant.  ☐

**d**  There's an animal.  ☐

**e**  There aren't any flowers.  ☐

**f**  There are five mushrooms.  ☐

**15**  **Write Y = Yes or N = No. Then ask and answer.**

**VALUES**

Play outside.
Play safe!

①

Me ☐  My friend ☐

Play at the playground.

②

Me ☐  My friend ☐

Play in the streets.

③

Me ☐  My friend ☐

Play at night.

④

Me ☐  My friend ☐

Play by yourself.

⑤

Me ☐  My friend ☐

Play with friends.

⑥

Me ☐  My friend ☐

Play in the hot sun.

Do you play at the playground?

Yes, I do.

 **16** What do you know?

**17**  Count and write. Then listen and check your answers.

+ (plus)    – (minus)    = (equals)

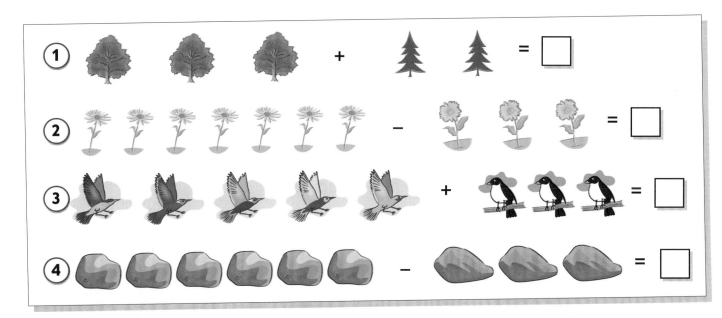

**1**  🌳 🌳 🌳  +  🌲 🌲  =  ☐

**2**  🌼 🌼 🌼 🌼 🌼 🌼 🌼  –  🌻 🌻 🌻  =  ☐

**3**  🐦 🐦 🐦 🐦 🐦  +  🐦 🐦 🐦  =  ☐

**4**  🪨 🪨 🪨 🪨 🪨 🪨  –  🪨 🪨 🪨  =  ☐

**18** Read the number puzzles. Then write the answer.

**1**

Three birds plus one spider.

How many legs?

☐

**2**

Two insects minus one cat.

How many legs?

☐

Can do simple sums and number puzzles

**19**   **Make a bug. Talk to a friend.**

Look at my bug. It's an insect. It has six legs and two wings.

My bug is a spider. It's blue. It has eight legs.

1 **Think** about bugs.
2 **Choose** a bug.
3 **Make** a bug.
4 **Talk** about your bug.

HOME SCHOOL LINK

Talk to your family about bugs.

**20**  A:28 **Listen.**

PHONICS

①  **hair**    ②  **year**

**21**  A:29 **Listen and blend the sounds.**

**22**   **Underline** *air* **and** *ear*. **Read the sentences aloud.**

1   This girl has long hair.

2   Sit down on the chair.

3   I can hear with my ear.

4   A pair is near the chair.

**23**  **Listen and number.**

**a**

**b**

**c**

**d**

**e**

**f**

**g**

**h**

**24**  **Play a guessing game. Ask and answer.**

Are there any trees?

Is there a rainbow?

Picture d!

Yes, there are.

No, there isn't.

**25**  **Draw the view from your window. Ask and answer.**

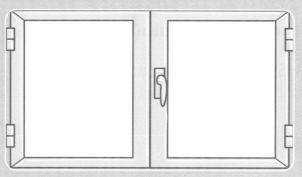

Are there any trees?

Yes, there are five trees.

Are there any flowers?

No, there aren't.

I can identify common nature words.
I can ask and answer about how many there are.
I can do simple sums and number puzzles.

26  **Spot the differences. Cover a picture. Ask a friend.**

Is there a rainbow?

No, there isn't.

Are there any flowers?

Yes, there are. There are 13 flowers.

Now go to Poptropica English World

# Wider World 1

## Birthdays around the world

**1**  **What do you know?**

**2**  **Listen and read.**
A:31

Hi, I'm Lucy. I'm from the United States. Today's my birthday. I'm nine. Look at my birthday cake. There are nine candles. My friends and family sing "Happy Birthday," and I blow out the candles. I love birthdays!

**1**

candle

cake

**2**

piñata

My name's Diego, and I'm eight. I'm from Mexico. Look! It's my birthday party. There's a big *piñata* with candy inside. We break the *piñata*, and the candy falls out.

Can understand texts about other children's birthdays

banchan

seaweed soup

Hello. I'm Yoon-ji, and I'm from Korea. I'm eight today. For my birthday, I have a big breakfast in the morning with seaweed soup and a lot of different dishes called *banchan*. Yum!

**3 Circle.**

1 Diego's ( eight / nine ).

2 There are ( nine / ten ) candles on Lucy's cake.

3 There's ( candy / cake ) in the *piñata*.

4 Yoon-ji likes ( cake / soup ) on her birthday.

**4**  **Ask and answer.**

1 How old are you?

2 Is there a cake at your birthday party?

3 Are there candles?

4 Do you have a piñata?

5 Is there any candy?

Tell the Class

# 2 Me

**1** What do you know?

**2** (A:32) Listen and find. What's missing?

dark eyebrows

blond hair

curly hair

gray hair

glasses

a black mustache

a short beard

blue eyes

brown eyes

red hair

**3** (A:33) Listen and number.

**4** (A:34) Listen and say.

a

b

c

d

e

f

g

h

Can identify physical characteristics

**5**  **Listen and chant.**

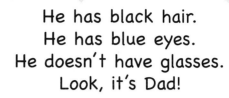

He has black hair.
He has blue eyes.
He doesn't have glasses.
Look, it's Dad!

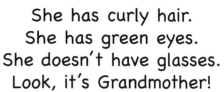

She has curly hair.
She has green eyes.
She doesn't have glasses.
Look, it's Grandmother!

**LOOK!**
A:37

| I | have | glasses. |
| | don't have | dark eyebrows. |
| He She | has | |
| | doesn't have | |

**6** Play a guessing game.

He has red hair. He doesn't have glasses.

Peter!

**7**  Listen and check.

long eyelashes ☐

black beard ☐

pink lips ☐

white teeth ☐

red nose ☐

big chin ☐

big mouth ☐

**8**  Listen and find. Then sing.

Who am I? Who am I? Who am I?

Do you have curly hair?

Yes, I do. Yes, I do. Yes, I do.

Do you have a big chin?

No, I don't.

Do you have a big mouth?

Yes, I do. Yes, I do. Yes, I do.

Do you have a red nose?

No, I don't.

Do you have pink lips?

Yes, I do. Yes, I do. Yes, I do.

Do you have long eyelashes?

No, I don't.

Who am I? Who am I? Who am I?

Can identify more physical characteristics

A:41

| **Do** you **have** | long eyelashes? | **Yes**, I do. |
| | | **No**, I **don't**. |
| **Does** he/she **have** | curly hair? | **Yes**, he/she **does**. |
| | | **No**, he/she **doesn't**. |

**9**  A:42 **Listen and number.**

a

Paulo

b

Arisu

c

Eva

**10** **Look at Activity 9. Ask and answer.**

SPEAKING

Does Paulo have a red nose?

Yes, he does.

**Talk about the pictures. Then listen and read.**

12  **Role-play the story.**

**13 Read the story again and circle.**

1   ( Captain Conrad / Dr. Bones ) is on the bus.

2   Dr. Bones has ( brown hair / blond hair ).

3   She doesn't have ( a beard / glasses ).

4   ( Shirley Homeland / Dr. Bones ) has spots.

5   Everyone on the bus has ( glasses / spots ).

6   Dr. Bones ( can / can't ) help them find the tifftiff plant.

**VALUES**

Have good habits. Keep clean and healthy.

**14** Write *Y* = Yes or *N* = No. Then ask and answer.

1   Me ☐ My friend ☐
Cut your fingernails.

2   Me ☐ My friend ☐
Brush your teeth every day.

3   Me ☐ My friend ☐
Take a bath or shower every day.

4   Me ☐ My friend ☐
Wash your hands before and after eating.

5   Me ☐ My friend ☐
Eat a lot of vegetables.

6   Me ☐ My friend ☐
Cover your mouth when you cough.

Do you cut your fingernails?

Yes, I do.

**15**   **What do you know?**

**16**   **A:44** **Listen, read, and stick.**

*Australian animals*

**marsupial**
The kangaroo has a big body and a pouch. It has two long legs and two short arms. It has a long tail and big feet. It has a small head. It has big ears and small eyes.

**reptile**
This is a blind snake. It has a long body and a small head. It has a small mouth and two very small eyes. It can't see.

**bird**
This bird is an emu. It has a big body and two wings. It has two long legs. It has a long neck and a small head. It has big eyes and long eyelashes.

**Stick**

**17**  **A:45** **Listen and circle T = True or F = False.**

**1**  T / F  **2**  T / F  **3**  T / F  **4**  T / F  **5**  T / F  **6**  T / F

**18** **Choose an animal and describe it to your friend.**

koala

small eyes
big ears
fur
black nose
pouch

The koala has...

wombat

small eyes
small ears
brown fur
short legs

The wombat has...

**19 Make a poster. Talk to a friend.**

1 **Think** about animals in your country.
2 **Choose** some animals.
3 **Make** a poster of animals in your country.
4 **Talk** about your poster.

Show your poster to your family.

This animal has four legs. It has a long tail and spots.

This animal is small. It has an orange head and wings.

 **20 Listen.**

PHONICS

 ① **say**   ② **dinner**

 **21 Listen and blend the sounds.**

 **22 Underline *ay* and *er*. Read the sentences aloud.**

**1** We want fish for dinner.

**2** Look! There's a letter.

**3** We play all day in the summer.

**4** I play with my toy hammer.

**23 Read and check (✓).**

**1**   eyebrows ☐
    glasses ☐
    a big nose ☐
    a beard ☐

**2**   a beard ☐
    a red nose ☐
    a mustache ☐
    glasses ☐

**3**   eyebrows ☐
    a red nose ☐
    curly hair ☐
    glasses ☐

**24** 🎧 A:48 **Listen and check (✓). Then check with a friend.**

This is his grandfather. He has a beard, but he doesn't have a mustache.

**I CAN**

I can describe people's physical characteristics.
I can talk about good habits and keeping clean and healthy.
I can describe Australian animals.

25  **Choose. Then play.**

1 Jonas

2 Jenny

3 Bill

4 Susan

5 Marco

6 David

7 Alice

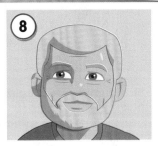
8 Joe

9 Peter

10 Lucy

11 Adam

12 Rosie

13 Jack

14 Julie

15 Sally

16 Betty

Do you have brown hair?

Yes, I do.

Do you have dark eyebrows?

Yes, I do.

Are you Bill?

Yes!

**Now go to Poptropica English World**

**Lesson 10**

Can use what I have learned in Unit 2

1 Play a guessing game.

Can talk about nature and physical characteristics

# 3 Pets

1 What do you know?

2 🎧 A:49 Listen and find. What's missing?

tail

beak

wings

feathers

claws

fins

whiskers

skin

fur

paws

3 🎧 A:50 Listen and number.

4 🎧 A:51 Listen and say.

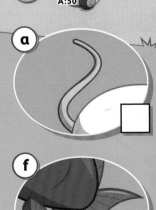

a □
b □
c □
d □

f □
g □
h □
i □

Can identify animal body parts

**5**  A:52 / A:53 **Listen and chant.**

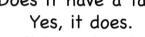
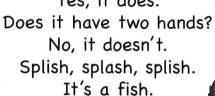

Does it have two eyes?
Yes, it does.
Does it have four legs?
No, it doesn't.
Does it have a tail?
Yes, it does.
Does it have two hands?
No, it doesn't.
Splish, splash, splish.
It's a fish.

## LOOK!

A:54

| What | **does** it | look like? |
| | **do** they | |
| It | **has** | a tail. |
| | **doesn't have** | wings. |
| They | **have** | whiskers. |
| | **don't have** | fins. |

**6**  **Look at the animals in the chant. Ask and answer.**

What does it look like?

It's green. It has four legs and big eyes.

It's a frog.

**e**

**j**

**7**  **Listen and number. Then say.**

**a**  ☐
scary

**b**  ☐
a hard shell

**c**  ☐
fast

**d**  ☐
soft fur

**e**  ☐
cute

**f**  ☐
sharp claws

**g**  ☐
slow

SONG

**8**  **Listen and write. Then sing.**

**Chorus:**

Pet, pets, pets are a lot of fun!

There's a pet for everyone!

Do you have a turtle? Yes, I do.

It has a $^1$_____ and is so $^2$_____.

It's a lot of fun! It's a lot of fun!

**(Chorus)**

Do you have a cat? No, I don't.

Do you have a dog? No, I don't.

**(Chorus)**

Do you have a hamster? Yes, I do!

It has $^3$_____ and is so $^4$_____.

It's a lot of fun! It's a lot of fun!

Can identify animal characteristics

**LOOK!**

| Do you **have** a dog? | **Yes**, I **do**. It's cute. | **Does** it **have** soft fur? | **Yes**, it does. |
|---|---|---|---|
| | **No**, I **don't**. | | **No**, it **doesn't**. |

**9**   **Choose a pet. Ask and answer.**

1

paws, tail, claws, soft fur

2

hard shell, slow, fun

3

beak, feathers, wings, fast

4

soft fur, short tail, cute, fast

5
fins, tail, small

6
no legs, long, scary

> My pet has wings. It's fast.

> Do you have a bird?

> Yes, I do.

**WRITING**

**10** **Write.**

**My pet**

Animal: tarantula
Name: Boris
Home: Arizona
Age: three years old
Color: brown
Legs: eight
Food: insects

Hi. I'm Alex, and I have a pet. It's a
¹_____, and it's from Arizona.
Its name is Boris. It's ²_____ old.
It's brown. It doesn't have a tail. It has
eight ³_____.
It likes to eat ⁴_____.
Some people say it's scary.
I say it's cute and very smart.
I love my pet tarantula.

**Talk about the pictures. Then listen and read.**

1. The trickster has the wabberjock! Please help me!

2. What does the wabberjock look like?

   It has soft fur and a long tail.

3. Does it have sharp teeth?

   No, it doesn't.

   Aarrgghh!

4. Is it very big?

   No, it's small.

   Ow! Ow! Ow!

5. Is it...? Is it...? Is it the wabberjock?!

   Ooooh! It's beautiful!

6. Good job! You have the wabberjock!

   Hooray!

12  **Role-play the story.**

**13 Read and match.**

1  Does the wabberjock have spots?     a  Yes, it is.

2  Does it have sharp teeth?            b  No, it doesn't.

3  Is it big?                           c  Yes, it does.

4  Is it beautiful?                     d  It's pink.

5  Does it have a long tail?            e  No, it's small.

6  What color is it?                    f  Yes, it does.

VALUES

Take care of your pet.

**14**  **Write Y = Yes or N = No.
Then ask and answer.**

① Me ☐ My friend ☐
Feed your pet every day.

② Me ☐ My friend ☐
Give your pet fresh water.

③ Me ☐ My friend ☐
Take your pet to the vet.

④ Me ☐ My friend ☐
Keep your pet clean.

⑤ Me ☐ My friend ☐
Give your pet exercise.

⑥ Me ☐ My friend ☐
Clean your pet's home.

Do you feed your pet every day?

Yes, I do.

**What do you know?**

  **Listen and read. Then stick.**

A:60

1 First, there are small eggs.
2 Next, there are caterpillars. They have a lot of legs and big eyes.
3 Then there are cocoons. Cocoons are cases around the caterpillars' bodies.

4 Finally, there are butterflies. What do they look like? They have wings with many colors. They have stripes or spots.

( eggs )   ( caterpillars )   ( cocoons )   ( butterflies )

  **Listen and read. Then write.**

A:61

First, there are small eggs in the water.

Then the tadpoles are big. They have two legs now and long tails. They can swim fast.

Next, there are small tadpoles. They have long tails. They don't have legs.

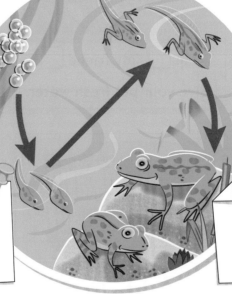

Finally, there are young frogs. They have four legs now. They have big eyes and big mouths. They can jump.

**1**  Where are the eggs? They're _____.

**2**  Do small tadpoles have short tails? No, they have _____.

**3**  Do big tadpoles have four legs? No, they have _____.

**4**  What can frogs do? They _____.

Can understand short texts about animal life cycles

**18**   Make a butterfly life cycle wheel.
Talk to a friend.

1 **Think** about the life cycle of a butterfly.
2 **Prepare** and draw each stage.
3 **Make** a butterfly life cycle wheel.
4 **Talk** about the butterfly life cycle.

# The life cycle of a butterfly

Look! First, there are small eggs.

**HOME SCHOOL LINK**

Show your life cycle wheel to your family.

**19**  A:62 **Listen.**

① **tea**

② **oil**

**20**  A:63 **Listen and blend the sounds.**

**21**  **Underline *ea* and *oi*. Read the sentences aloud.**

1   I have a silver coin.

2   Eat a peach.

3   Put oil on the foil.

4   Join me for leaf tea.

**22** 🎧 A:64 **Listen and number.**

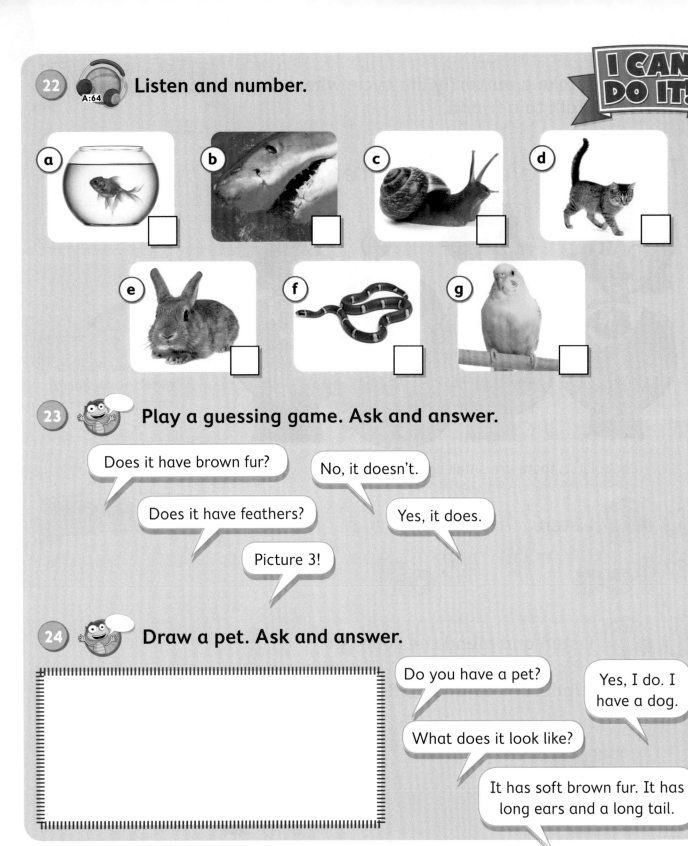

a

b

c

d

e

f

g

**23** **Play a guessing game. Ask and answer.**

Does it have brown fur?

No, it doesn't.

Does it have feathers?

Yes, it does.

Picture 3!

**24** **Draw a pet. Ask and answer.**

Do you have a pet?

Yes, I do. I have a dog.

What does it look like?

It has soft brown fur. It has long ears and a long tail.

## I CAN

I can talk about pets and their characteristics.

I can talk about taking care of my pet.

I can understand short texts about animal life cycles.

Can assess what I have learned in Unit 3

25   **Draw or write. Then play.**

## My house

yard

| | |
|---|---|
| bathroom | bedroom 2 |
| dining room | kitchen |
| bedroom 1 | living room |

yard

## My friend's house

yard

| | |
|---|---|
| bathroom | bedroom 2 |
| dining room | kitchen |
| bedroom 1 | living room |

yard

Is there a pet in the bathroom?

Yes, there is.

Does it have legs?

No, it doesn't.

Is it a snake?

Yes, it is.

Now go to Poptropica
English World

# Wider World 2

## Do you like pets?

**1**  **What do you know?**

**2**  **Listen and read.**

My name's Dagang. I'm from China. I have a pet rabbit. His name's Baobao. He's white, and he has long ears. His fur is very soft. He doesn't like pineapples. He likes apples and salad. I love my pet rabbit.

My name's Rika, and I'm from Japan. I have a pet hamster. Her name's Momo. She's two years old. She has small ears and a small tail. She likes apples and nuts. She can run fast in the hamster wheel. She's so cute. I love hamsters!

**3** **Match.**

| | | | |
|---|---|---|---|
| 1 | The turtle | a | likes fish and cheese. |
| 2 | The rabbit | b | likes apples and nuts. |
| 3 | The hamster | c | likes apples and eggs. |
| 4 | The cat | d | likes apples and salad. |

Can understand texts about other children's pets

**3**

I'm Pedro, and I'm from Colombia. I have a pet cat. Her name's Polly, and she's nine years old. She's white. She likes fish and cheese, but she doesn't like fruit. I love Polly.

**4**

I'm Jane, and I'm from Australia. I have a pet turtle. His name's Bruno. He has a small head and four strong legs. He's 15 years old. He has a very hard shell. He's big, and he likes apples and eggs.

**4** **Ask and answer.**

parrot

iguana

duck

spider

1    Do you like these pets?

2    Why do you like them?

3    What's your favorite pet?

Tell the Class

**Wider World 2**

Can ask and answer about pets

# 4 Home

1  **What do you know?**

2  **Listen and find. What's missing?**

A:66

stove

picture

trash can

shower

window

computer

plant

TV

sofa

3  **Listen and match.**

A:67

4  **Listen and say.**

A:68

1

2

3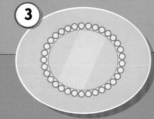

4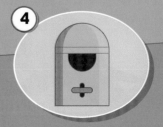

a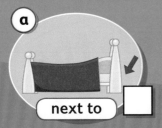

**next to** ☐

b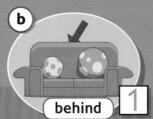

**behind** 1

c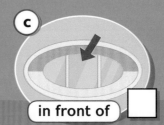

**in front of** ☐

d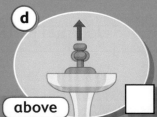

**above** ☐

**48** **Lesson 1**

Can identify home furnishings and where they are

**5**  **Listen and chant.**

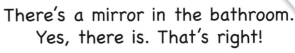

There's a mirror in the bathroom.
Yes, there is. That's right!

There's a picture above the bed.
Oops! There isn't. No, no, no.

There are plants behind the sofa.
Yes, there are. That's right!

There's a mirror above the sofa.
Oops! There isn't. No, no, no.

**LOOK!**

A:71

| There's a plant | in the living room. |
|---|---|
| There are two plants | |
| The plant is/It's | below the mirror. |
| The plants are/They're | |

**6**  **Listen and circle the things you hear. Then say.**

A:72

There's a computer on the table.

**Lesson 2**                    Can talk about where things are in a room   **49**

**7**  **Listen and number. Then say.**

**a** toothbrush

**b** towels

**c** pots

**d** blankets

**e** comb

**f** shelf

**g** pans

**h** plates

**8**  **Listen and circle. Then sing.**

**Chorus:**
Messy house, messy rooms everywhere,
With messy things here, and messy things there.
Behind, below, above, there.
Clean up, clean up everywhere.

Where are the ( 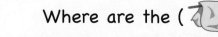 )?
Are they on the shelf? No, they aren't!
They're next to the chair.

**(Chorus)**

Where's the (  )?
Is it above the sink? No, it isn't.
It's under the plates.

**(Chorus)**

Where are the ( )?
Are they in the closet? No, they aren't!
They're behind the plant.

**(Chorus)**

Can identify household items

| | | | |
|---|---|---|---|
| **Is** the computer in the bedroom? | **Yes**, it **is**. | **Are** the plates on the shelf? | **Yes**, they **are**. |
| | **No**, it **isn't**. It's in the living room. | | **No**, they **aren't**. They**'re** in the sink. |

**9** Choose two rooms and stick. Then say.

> My favorite room is the bathroom. There's a plant next to the tub.

**10**  Listen and read. Then write.

 **READING**

> There are two beds in my bedroom — my bed and my brother's bed. There's a pink blanket on my bed. There's a big closet next to my brother's bed. There are toys on the shelf in the closet. There isn't a computer in the bedroom. It's in the living room. I have a cat named Tilly. There's a picture of Tilly above my bed. Do you like my bedroom?

**1** How many beds are there? _____

**2** Where's the pink blanket? _____

**3** Are the toys under the bed? _____

**4** Is the computer in the bedroom? _____

**5** Is the picture of Tilly above the bed? _____

**Talk about the pictures. Then listen and read.**

12   **Role-play the story.**

**13** **Look at the story. Find and write the number of the picture.**

a    Kim is next to the door. ☐

b    Fid is in front of the door. ☐

c    There's a trickster in the kitchen. ☐

d    Fid has the tifftiff plant. 2

e    The tifftiff plant is above Prod 1. ☐

f    The sofa is below the window. ☐

VALUES

Help at home.

**14**  **Write Y = Yes or N = No.**
**Then ask and answer.**

1   Me ☐   My friend ☐
Sweep the floor.

2   Me ☐   My friend ☐
Put away your toys.

3   Me ☐   My friend ☐
Dust the shelves.

4   Me ☐   My friend ☐
Dry the dishes.

5   Me ☐   My friend ☐
Take out the trash.

6   Me ☐   My friend ☐
Hang up your clothes.

Do you sweep the floor?

Yes, I do.

**15**  **What do you know?**

 **16**  **A:79** **Read. Then listen and answer.**

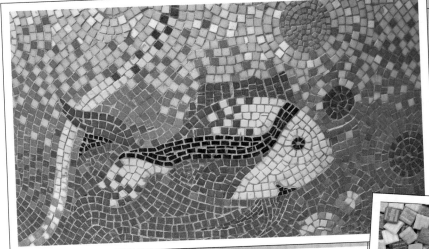

This is a mosaic. It's a picture that has small tiles, stones, or glass. It has squares, circles, rectangles, and triangles in different colors. There are mosaics on floors and on walls. They're very beautiful. Do you like mosaics?

tiles

stones

glass

1 ( Yes, they are. / No, they aren't. )

2 ( Yes, there are. / No, there aren't. )

3 ( Yes / No ). It's a _____ of a _____ .

**17** **Count the shapes and write.**

1 How many triangles are there? ☐

2 How many squares are there? ☐

3 How many circles are there? ☐

4 How many rectangles are there? ☐

Can understand a text about mosaics

**18**   **Make a mosaic picture. Talk to a friend.**

PROJECT

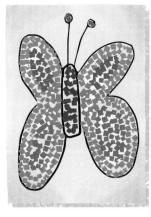

1 **Think** about a subject for a mosaic.
2 **Prepare** and draw a mosaic.
3 **Make** a mosaic.
4 **Talk** about your mosaic.

HOME SCHOOL LINK

Show your mosaic pictures to your family.

Look at my house! There are a lot of squares and triangles.

Look! It's a fish. It's blue, green, and purple.

PHONICS

**19**  **B:02** **Listen.**

① **cake**    ② **time**    ③ **home**

**20**  **B:03** **Listen and blend the sounds.**

**21**  **Underline *a_e*, *i_e*, and *o_e*. Read the sentences aloud.**

**1** The dog has a bone.

**2** I like cake!

**3** Dive under the wave.

**4** It's time to go home.

**22** **Look. Then write *Y* = Yes or *N* = No.**

**1** There's a plant on the table. __Y__

**2** There's a mirror above the bed. ___

**3** There's a shower behind the door. ___

**4** There are blankets in the closet. ___

**5** There's a trash can behind the stove. ___

**6** There's a computer in front of the window. ___

**7** There are pots and pans in front of the stove. ___

**8** There's a towel next to the sink. ___

**23**  **Play a memory game. Ask and answer.**

> Where's the plant?

> It's on the table.

**24**  **Draw your bedroom. Ask and answer.**

> Where's the closet?

> It's next to the door.

 **CAN**

I can identify household items.

I can talk about where things are in the home.

I can understand a text about mosaics.

In picture A, there's a plant next to the closet.

In picture B, the plant is next to the desk!

Now go to Poptropica English World

# Review  Units 3 and 4

**1** 🎧 **B:04** Listen and check (✓).

**1** ☐   **2** ☐   **3** ☐

**2** 😃 Ask and answer.

 **1**

 **2**

 **3**

 **4**

 **5**

 **6**

 Is the bird above the TV?

 Yes, it is.

Can talk about pets and where pets are

**3** **Read and underline four mistakes.**

This is my bedroom. It has a bed, a closet, a chair, a TV, and a lamp. There are two tables – a big table and a small table. The lamp is on the small table. It's next to the books. There are four books on top of the closet. I have a snake. It's in front of the closet. It's great!

**4** **Look and circle.**

1  There are plants ( behind / in front of ) the sink.

2  There's a picture ( above / next to ) the sofa.

3  There's a computer ( in front of / next to ) the sofa.

4  There are pans ( below / in ) the pots.

# 5 Clothes

**1** What do you know?

**2** B:05 Listen and find. What's missing?

a shirt

a polo shirt

a sweatsuit

shorts

a baseball cap

a belt

a uniform

a jacket

flip-flops

sneakers

**3** B:06 Listen and number.

**4** B:07 Listen and say.

a

b

c

d

e

g

h

i

j

k

Can identify clothing items

jeans

a sweatshirt

sandals

f

l

**5** B:08 / B:09 **Listen and chant.**

Hey, hey! What are you wearing?
I'm wearing a uniform.
Hey, hey! What are you wearing?
I'm wearing a sweatshirt.
Hey, hey! What are you wearing?
I'm wearing a baseball cap.
A baseball cap?
He's wearing my baseball cap!

## LOOK!
B:10

| What **are** you wear**ing**? | **I'm** wear**ing** | a baseball cap. sandals. |
|---|---|---|
| What**'s** he/she wear**ing**? | He**'s**/She**'s** wear**ing** | |
| **Are** you wear**ing** | a baseball cap? sandals? | **Yes**, I **am**. |
| | | **No**, I**'m not**. |
| **Is** he/she wear**ing** | | **Yes**, he/she **is**. |
| | | **No**, he/she **isn't**. |

**6** Look at Laurence Laundry, Fashionista, and PROD 2. Then ask and answer.

Look at Captain Conrad. What's he wearing?

He's wearing a uniform.

Is he wearing sandals?

No, he isn't.

**7** **B:11** Listen and number. Then say.

**a**  ( beanie ) ☐

**b**  ( hiking boots ) ☐

**c**  ( colorful ) ☐

**d**  ( fancy ) ☐

**e** 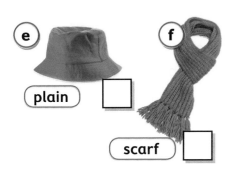 ( plain ) ☐

**f** ( scarf ) ☐

**g** 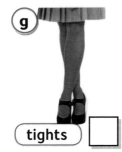 ( tights ) ☐

**h**  ( ski jacket ) ☐

**i**  ( wool sweater ) ☐

 **8** **B:12 / B:13** Listen and circle. Then sing.

**Chorus:**

Where's my red scarf? Where's my red scarf?

I have my (  ),

My beanie, and my ( ).

But not my red scarf! Not my red scarf!

My sister's in the bedroom. What's she wearing?

She's wearing my (  ).

Is she wearing my scarf? No, she isn't. No, no, no!

**(Chorus)**

My brother's in the garden. What's he wearing?

He's wearing my (   ).

Is he wearing my scarf? Yes, he is. Yes, yes, yes!

Can identify more clothing items and words that describe them

**9**   **Draw and color two favorite clothing items. Then say.**

| | | |
|---|---|---|
| This is | **my favorite** | scarf. |
| These are | | tights. |

I love my scarf/tights.

**Item 1**

This is my favorite scarf.
It's red and blue.

**Item 2**

**10**   **Listen and read. Then write.**

costume party

Hi. I'm Hilda. I'm a pirate. I'm wearing a plain white shirt and a black and red skirt. This is my favorite skirt. I'm wearing black shoes and white socks. Do you like my fancy hat?

I'm Ben. I'm a clown. My hair is orange. I'm wearing a big yellow T-shirt and big blue pants. These are my favorite shoes. And I love my colorful bow tie. Do you like it?

**1** She's _____.    **2** It's a _____.

**3** He's _____.    **4** It's a _____.

12   **Role-play the story.**

**13** **Read the story again and circle.**

1   ( The red trickster / Katy ) has the tifftiff plant.

2   The trickster is ( wearing / behind ) the blue skirt.

3   ( The red trickster / A red jacket ) is behind the jeans.

4   There's a ( fancy / plain ) dress.

5   ( Kim / Prod 2 ) has the red trickster.

6   Prod 2 is wearing ( a dress / a jacket ).

**14**  **Look and read. Then listen and write.**

**VALUES**

Be polite.

Please.

Excuse me.

Thank you.

You're welcome.

I'm sorry.

I'm happy for you.

1   When we get a present, we say, " _____ ."

2   When we hurt someone, we say, " _____ ."

3   When we ask for something, we say, " _____ ."

4   When someone says, "Thank you," we say, " _____ ."

5   When someone tells us good news, we say, " _____ ."

6   When we want to get someone's attention, we say, " _____ ."

**What do you know?**

 **Read. Then check (✓) the things you do.**

1  set the table ☐

2 clean my bedroom ☐

3 make my bed ☐

4  wash the dishes ☐

5 wash the car ☐

**17 Read and number the pictures.**

1 **Mom:** Amy, please set the table.

**Amy:** OK, Mom.

2 **Mom:** Wow, your bedroom is clean! Good job, Amy!

**Amy:** Thanks, Mom!

3 **Mom:** Amy, please make your bed.

**Amy:** Sorry, Mom. I'm busy with homework.

4 **Mom:** Amy, clean your bedroom, please.

**Amy:** I'm sorry, Mom.

5 **Mom:** Please, Amy. Wash the dishes.

**Amy:** OK, Mom!

Can identify household chores

**18** Make a chores chart. Talk to a friend.

## SAM'S CHORES

| Chores | Monday | Tuesday | Wednesday | Thursday | Friday |
|---|---|---|---|---|---|
| Set the table | | | | | |
| Clean my bedroom | | | | | |
| Put away my toys | | | | | |
| Make my bed | | | | | |
| Hang up my clothes | | | | | |
| Wash the dishes | | | | | |
| Wash the car | | | | | |

1 **Think** about your chores this week.
2 **Prepare** a list of your chores.
3 **Make** a chores chart.
4 **Talk** about your chores chart.

HOME SCHOOL LINK

Use your chores chart at home.

PHONICS

**19**   B:18 Listen.

① scarf ② skate ③ smell ④ snip
⑤ spoon ⑥ squid ⑦ star ⑧ swim

**20** B:19 Listen and blend the sounds.

**21** Underline *sc, sk, sn, squ, st,* and *sw*. Read the sentences aloud.

1 Look at the star!

2 Snip some hair.

3 See the squid swim.

4 Wear a scarf to skate.

**22** **Listen and match.**

**1** Rob    **2** Beth    **3** Harry    **4** Suzy    **5** Matt    **6** Lulu

a    b    c    d    e    f

**23** **Look at Activity 22. Play a guessing game. Ask and answer.**

Is he wearing a colorful scarf?

No, he isn't.

Is he wearing hiking boots?

Yes, he is.

It's Rob!

**24** **What are you wearing? Draw and write.**

I'm wearing a _____ and _____.

**I CAN**

I can ask and answer about what people are wearing.

I can use polite phrases in English.

I can make a chores chart.

**25**  **Stick. Then ask, answer, and draw.**

Are you wearing shorts?

Yes, I am.

Are you wearing a scarf?

No, I'm not.

Me

My friend

**26**  **Tell another friend.**

This is my favorite...

These are my favorite...

I love my...

Now go to Poptropica
English World

# Wider World 3
## School uniforms

**1**  **What do you know?**

**2**  **Listen and read.**

My name's Clara, and I'm from Mexico. In my school, we don't have uniforms. Here, I'm wearing a plain red T-shirt, black pants, and my favorite sneakers. They're black and very comfortable.

I'm Scott, and I'm from the United Kingdom. My school is in Oxford, and we have uniforms. I'm wearing a blue shirt, blue pants, and a blue jacket. I'm wearing my black school shoes.

**3** **Write C (Clara), S (Scott), E (Emma), or J (Jiaming).**

**1** She isn't wearing a uniform. She's wearing a pink shirt.

**2** He's wearing a uniform. He isn't wearing a jacket.

**3** She's wearing a T-shirt and sneakers.

**4** He isn't wearing sandals. He's wearing shoes.

Can understand texts about school uniforms

I'm Emma, and I'm from Canada. I'm not wearing a uniform. I'm wearing a pink shirt and my favorite jeans. I love my pink bag!

My name's Jiaming. I'm from China. We have uniforms in my school. I'm wearing a white shirt, blue shorts, black socks, and black sneakers. These are my favorite sneakers.

 **4** **Ask and answer.**

**1** What are you wearing?

**2** Are you wearing a uniform?

**3** Do you like uniforms?

Tell the Class

# 6 Sports

do taekwondo

1 ⭐ **What do you know?**

2 🎧 B:22 **Listen and find. What's missing?**

catch a ball

play tennis

run

play baseball

ride a bike

3 🎧 B:23 **Listen and number.**

4 🎧 B:24 **Listen and say.**

a

b

c

e

f

g

Can identify sports and abilities

play basketball

play soccer

d

h

5  **Listen and chant.**

B:25 / B:26

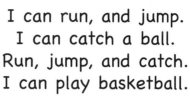

I can run, and jump.
I can catch a ball.
Run, jump, and catch.
I can play basketball.

I can run, and jump,
But I can't catch a ball.
Run, jump, and catch.
I can't play basketball.

**LOOK!**

B:27

| I/He/She | **can/can't** | run and jump. |
| | **can** | run, but I/he/she **can't** jump. |
| **Can** you/he/she play tennis? | **Yes,** | I/he/she | **can.** |
| | **No,** | | **can't.** |

6  **Listen and ✓ = can or ✗ = can't. Then ask and answer.**

B:28

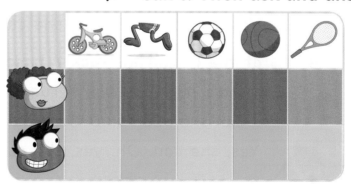

Can Kim run?

Yes, he can.

**7** Listen and number. Then say.

VOCABULARY

B:29

a

gym

b 
baseball field

c 
basketball court

d 
running track

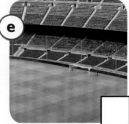
e
stadium

f

ski slope

g
beach

h
swimming pool

i
tennis court

j
soccer field

**8** Listen and circle. Then sing.

B:30 / B:31

SONG

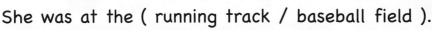

She was at the ( soccer field / basketball court ).
Can she play ( basketball / soccer )?
Can she? Can she? Can she?
Yes, she can. Oh, yes, she can.

She was at the ( running track / baseball field ).
Can she ( play baseball / run fast )?
Can she? Can she? Can she?
Yes, she can. Oh, yes, she can.

He was at the ( gym / beach ),
At the ( gym / beach ).
Can he ( climb / jump ) the rope?
Can he? Can he? Can he?
Yes, he can. Oh, yes, he can.

Can identify sports facilities

## LOOK!

| I/He/She | **was** at the gym. |
|---|---|
| | **wasn't** at the gym. I/He/She **was** at the baseball field. |

**9** B:33 **Listen and ✓ = was or ✗ = wasn't. Then say.**

**1**

**2**

**3**

**4**

> She wasn't at the beach. She was at the stadium.

**10**  B:34 **Listen and read. Then stick.**

 READING

Monday, July 1st

I was at the Aquaworld Festival to watch the dolphin show. It was a lot of fun! Dolphins can't walk or run, but they can swim 5 to 12 kilometers per hour and jump out of the water. They can jump through hoops and catch a ball. They have very strong fins. They are very smart animals. I love dolphins!

 Stick

**1** Dolphins can...

**2** Dolphins can't...

12   **Role-play the story.**

**13** **Read and match.**

1  Is PROD 2 strong?    a  Yes, he can. He's in the swimming pool.

2  Can PROD 2 play basketball?    b  No, he can't. He doesn't have wings.

3  Can PROD 1 swim?    c  Yes, he is.

4  Can PROD 1 run fast?    d  No, he can't, but he can play tennis.

5  Can PROD 1 fly?    e  Yes. He's good at catching.

6  Can PROD 2 catch?    f  No, he can't. He's slow.

**14**  **Write Y = Yes or N = No.**
**Then ask and answer.**

**VALUES**

Be active. Exercise every day.

**1**  Me ☐  My friend ☐
Go for a walk.

**2**  Me ☐  My friend ☐
Run.

**3**  Me ☐  My friend ☐
Ride your bike.

**4**  Me ☐  My friend ☐
Do push-ups.

**5**  Me ☐  My friend ☐
Play sports.

**6**  Me ☐  My friend ☐
Do taekwondo.

Do you go for a walk?

Yes, I do.

**15**  **What do you know?**

**16**  **Listen and do.**

# Stay fit! Stay healthy!

**1** Stretch your arms up.

**2** Bend your knees.

**3** Twist your body to the left.

**4** Twist your body to the right.

**5** Turn around.

**17** **Which activities are healthy? Write ✓ or X.**

**1** ☐
Exercise every day.

**2**  ☐
Ride your bike to school.

**3** ☐
Drink soda.

**4**  ☐
Eat a lot of fruit.

**5**  ☐
Play computer games.

**6** ☐
Drink a lot of water.

**7**  ☐
Go to bed early.

**8**  ☐
Eat cake and ice cream.

**18**  Make a healthy living poster.
Talk to a friend.

1 **Think** about healthy living.
2 **Choose** examples of healthy living.
3 **Make** a healthy living poster.
4 **Talk** about your poster.

Show your poster to your family.

**19**  **Listen.**

PHONICS

1 **black**  2 **flag**  3 **glass**
4 **plate**  5 **sleep**

**20**  **Listen and blend the sounds.**

**21** **Underline *bl, fl, gl, pl,* and *sl*. Read the sentences aloud.**

1 I want a glass of pink milk.

2 Go to sleep.

3 There's plum jam on the spoon.

4 Look at the black flag.

**Lesson 8**  Can make a healthy living poster / Can pronounce the sounds bl, fl, gl, pl, and sl  **79**

| |  | | | | | | |
|---|---|---|---|---|---|---|---|
| Jake | | | | | | | |
| Tina | | | | | | | |
| Simon | | | | | | | |
| Donna | | | | | | | |

23 **Play a guessing game. Look at Activity 22. Ask and answer.**

He can ride a bike, but he can't play baseball.

Can he play soccer?

Yes, he can.

It's Jack.

24 **Mime a sport. Ask and answer.**

Are you at the basketball court?

Yes, I am.

You can play basketball!

I can identify sports and abilities.

I can ask and answer about what people can and can't do.

I can make a healthy living poster.

# Quiz time!

## How active are you?

**1 Read the questions to your friend and circle Yes or No.**

| | | |
|---|---|---|
| 1 | Can you play soccer? | ( Yes / No ) |
| 2 | Can you run fast? | ( Yes / No ) |
| 3 | Can you ride a bike? | ( Yes / No ) |
| 4 | Can you swim? | ( Yes / No ) |
| 5 | Do you go walking every day? | ( Yes / No ) |
| 6 | Do you do push-ups? | ( Yes / No ) |
| 7 | Do you do taekwondo? | ( Yes / No ) |
| 8 | Do you go jogging on the weekend? | ( Yes / No ) |
| 9 | Do you go to the swimming pool sometimes? | ( Yes / No ) |
| 10 | Do you go to the gym sometimes? | ( Yes / No ) |

**2 Count the Yes answers and read the results to your friend.**

**1–3 Yes answers:**

Oh, dear! You are not very active. Sports are good for you. Walk to school or ride your bike in the park. Exercise every day. It's fun!

**4–6 Yes answers:**

Good job! You are active. You play a lot of sports, but do you exercise every day? You can do push-ups before school and go jogging on the weekend. Exercise is fun!

**7–10 Yes answers:**

Fantastic! You are very active. You are fit and healthy, too. You exercise every day. Ask your friends to exercise with you. Have fun!

**Now go to Poptropica English World**

# Review  Units 5 and 6

**1** 🎧 **B:40** Listen and number.

**a**

**b**

**c**

**2** Read and circle.

**1**

She can ( play tennis /
do taekwondo ).

She's wearing
( shoes / sneakers ).

She's wearing
( shorts / a skirt ).

**2**

He's wearing a
( white uniform /
sweatsuit ).

He can ( play baseball /
do taekwondo ).

He has a black
( belt / scarf ).

**3**

Her favorite sport is
( soccer / tennis ).

She's wearing
( tights / long socks ).

She's wearing
( hiking boots /
soccer boots ).

Can talk about clothes and sports

**Play a guessing game.**

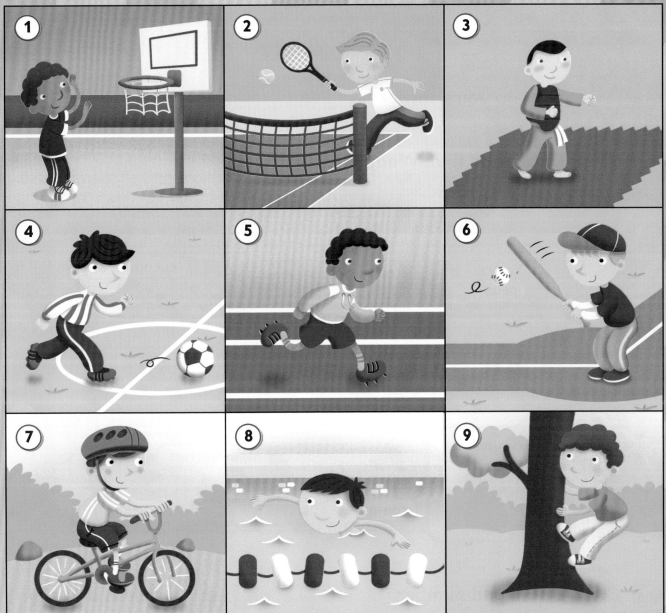

Are you wearing shorts?

Are you at the gym?

Are you wearing a baseball cap?

Can you play baseball?

Yes, I am.

No, I'm not.

Yes, I am.

Yes, I can!

# 7 Food

**1** ⭐ What do you know?

**2** 🎧 B:41 Listen and find. What's missing?

peas

mangoes

cucumbers

carrots

plums

oranges

peaches

potatoes

strawberries

tomatoes

beans

**3** 🎧 B:42 Listen and number.

**4** 🎧 B:43 Listen and say.

a    b    c    d    e

g    h    i    j

Can identify fruit and vegetables

**5**  B:44 / B:45 **Listen and chant.**

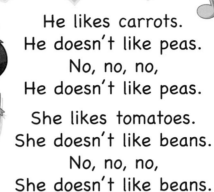

He likes carrots.
He doesn't like peas.
No, no, no,
He doesn't like peas.

She likes tomatoes.
She doesn't like beans.
No, no, no,
She doesn't like beans.

**LOOK!** B:46

| Do you | like | peas? | Yes, I do. |
| --- | --- | --- | --- |
| | | | No, I don't. |
| Does he/she | | | Yes, he/she does. |
| | | | No, he/she doesn't. |

**6**  B:47 **Listen again. Then ask and answer.**

Captain Conrad    Katy    Kim    PROD 1

Does Captain Conrad like mangoes?

Yes, he does.

f

k

**7** 🎧 B:48 **Listen and number. Then say.**

**a** broccoli

**b** lettuce

**c** spinach

**d** cabbage

**e** pears

**f** apricots

**g** avocados

**h** cherries

**8** 🎧 B:49 / B:50 **Listen and circle. Then sing.**

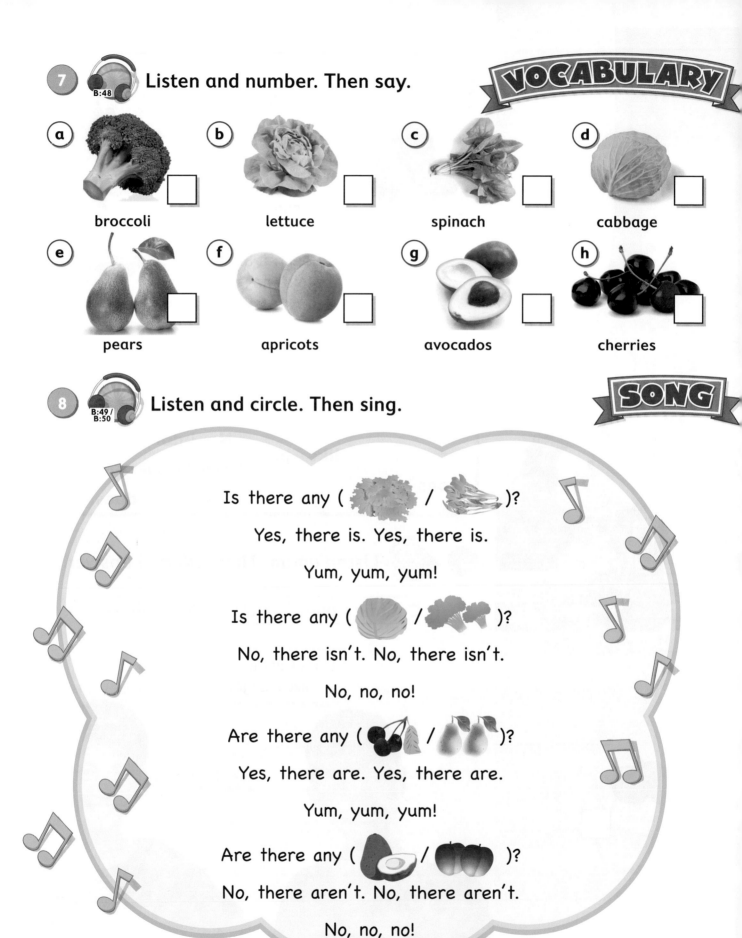

Is there any ( / )?

Yes, there is. Yes, there is.

Yum, yum, yum!

Is there any ( / )?

No, there isn't. No, there isn't.

No, no, no!

Are there any ( / )?

Yes, there are. Yes, there are.

Yum, yum, yum!

Are there any ( / )?

No, there aren't. No, there aren't.

No, no, no!

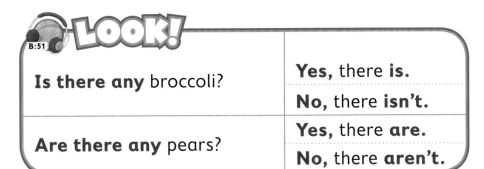

## 7

## LOOK!

B:51

| Is there any broccoli? | **Yes,** there **is.** |
| | **No,** there **isn't.** |
| Are there any pears? | **Yes,** there **are.** |
| | **No,** there **aren't.** |

9   **Choose five foods and stick. Then ask and answer.**

Are there any carrots?

Yes, there are.

 Stick

10   B:52 **Listen and read. Then write.**

 READING

**Lisa Martin Astronaut**

**Reporter:** Hello, Lisa. Do you have breakfast in space?
**Lisa:** Yes, I do. Breakfast, lunch, and dinner.
**Reporter:** Is there any fruit?
**Lisa:** Yes, there is. I eat strawberries for breakfast. They're my favorite! I also eat yogurt.
**Reporter:** Do you have pears and avocados?
**Lisa:** We have pears, but we don't have avocados.
**Reporter:** Are there any vegetables?
**Lisa:** Yes, there are. I like beans, but I don't like spinach.
**Reporter:** Thank you, Lisa.

**1** Does Lisa like strawberries? _____

**2** Are there any avocadoes? _____

**3** Does she have any yogurt? _____

**4** Does she like spinach? _____

11  B:53 **Talk about the pictures. Then listen and read.**

 STORY

12  **Role-play the story.**

Can understand a simple story / Can role-play a story

**13** **Match and write.**

1 Ben Beamaway has            a   on a shelf.

2 Kim loves                   b   a strawberry and an egg.

3 Katy doesn't like         c   sorry.

4 The tifftiff plant is       d   eggs.

5 PROD 1 is                  e   strawberries.

**VALUES**

Stay healthy. Eat more fruit and vegetables.

**14**  **Write Y = Yes or N = No. Then ask and answer.**

| | | | Me | My friend |
|---|---|---|---|---|
| 1 | corn | ☺ | ☐ | ☐ |
| 2 | avocado | ☺ | ☐ | ☐ |
| 3 | pizza | 😐 | ☐ | ☐ |
| 4 | orange juice | ☺ | ☐ | ☐ |
| 5 | fries | 😐 | ☐ | ☐ |
| 6 | burger | 😐 | ☐ | ☐ |
| 7 | bananas | ☺ | ☐ | ☐ |
| 8 | soda | 😐 | ☐ | ☐ |

Do you like corn?

Yes, I do.

**Lesson 6**    *Can understand details of a story / Can talk about staying healthy and eating more fruit and vegetables*    **89**

**15**  **What do you know?**

**16**  B:54 **Listen and read. Then put these foods in the correct place.**

chicken   bananas   cereal   cucumber   milk   chocolate

Do you like healthy food? Look at the food groups. Pasta, bread, and cereal are in the yellow group. You can eat grains every day. Fruit and vegetables are in the green group. You can also eat fruit and vegetables every day. These are very good for you. Eggs, meat, and fish are proteins. These are in the pink group. Cheese and yogurt are dairy foods. They're in the blue group. Cakes and candy are in the purple group. Don't eat too many fats and sugars. They aren't healthy.

**17**  **Say the word. Find the food group.**

 Milk.    Dairy!

**18**   Make a healthy food plate.
Talk to a friend.

1 **Think** about healthy food.
2 **Draw** or find examples of healthy food.
3 **Make** a healthy food plate.
4 **Talk** about your food plate.

Show your healthy food plate to your family.

I like to eat a lot of fruit and vegetables.

**19**  **Listen.**
B:55

① **brown** ② **crab** ③ **drop** ④ **frog**
⑤ **green** ⑥ **press** ⑦ **string** ⑧ **train**

**20**  **Listen and blend the sounds.**
B:56

**21**  **Underline** *br, cr, dr, fr, gr, pr, str,* and *tr*. **Read the sentences aloud.**

1 Press to go up.

2 Look at the green frog.

3 The crab is brown.

4 Pull the train with the string.

**22** **Look and write.**

avocados   broccoli   cherries   cucumbers   lettuce
mangoes   oranges   plums   strawberries   tomatoes

1 _____  ☐
2 _____  ☐
3 _____  ☐
4 _____  ☐
5 _____  ☐
6 _____  ☐
7 _____  ☐
8 _____  ☐
9 _____  ☐
10 _____  ☐

**23** **Look at Activity 22. Listen and ✓ or ✗.**

**24** **What do you like? Write a shopping list. Then ask and answer.**

1 I like apples. _____
2 _____
3 _____
4 _____
5 _____
6 _____

Do you like tomatoes?

No, I don't.

**I CAN**

I can identify fruit and vegetables.
I can ask and answer about food likes and dislikes.
I can understand a text about food groups.

25  **Spot the differences. Ask and answer.**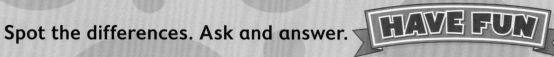

**A**

**B**

Are there any carrots?

Yes, there are.

Is there any lettuce?

No, there isn't.

26 **Write about the differences.**

**In Picture A:**

There aren't any mangoes.

_____

_____

_____

_____

_____

**In Picture B:**

There are mangoes.

_____

_____

_____

_____

_____

**Now go to Poptropica
English World**

**Lesson 10**

Can use what I have learned in Unit 7

# Wider World 4
## Food around the world

**1** ⭐ **What do you know?**

**2** 🎧 **B:58** **Listen and read.**

I'm Andrea. I'm from Argentina. I don't like potatoes, but I like meat. My favorite dinner is *asado*, or barbecue. I also like chocolate sandwiches. They aren't healthy, but I love them.

asado

My name's Zeki, and I'm from Turkey. These fantastic pastries have nuts in them. They aren't very healthy, but I also like fruit. I like chicken and vegetables, but I don't like fish.

pastries

**3** **Match.**

| | | | |
|---|---|---|---|
| **1** | Berta | **a** | likes chicken, but doesn't like fish. |
| **2** | Kay | **b** | likes pasta and chocolate ice cream. |
| **3** | Zeki | **c** | likes meat, but she doesn't like potatoes. |
| **4** | Andrea | **d** | likes rice and peas, but doesn't like pumpkin soup. |

Can understand texts about food likes and dislikes

**3**

My name's Kay. I'm from Jamaica. My favorite lunch is jerk chicken with rice and peas. It's a traditional dish. Yum! I also like meat patties. I like vegetables, but I don't like pumpkin soup.

jerk chicken

meat patties

**4**

I'm Berta, and I'm from Italy. My favorite dinner is pasta or pizza with cheese and tomatoes. I also like ice cream. Chocolate ice cream is my favorite!

ice cream

**4**  **Ask and answer.**

**1** Does Andrea like *asado*?

**2** Does Zeki like pastries?

**3** Does Kay like pumpkin soup?

**4** Does Berta like ice cream?

**5** What's your favorite food?

Tell the Class

# 8 Things we do

**1**  What do you know?

**2**  C:02 Listen and find. What's missing?

**3**  C:03 Listen and number.

listening to music

walking

 a

 b

 c

 d

 e

 f

 g

 h

 i

reading

drinking

eating

dancing

**4**  C:04 Listen and say.

**96** Lesson 1

Can identify actions and activities

sleeping

doing homework

cleaning

**5** **Listen and chant.**

C:05 / C:06

What are you doing?
I'm drinking, I'm drinking.
What are you doing?
I'm cleaning, I'm cleaning.
What are they doing?
They're sleeping, they're sleeping.

**LOOK!**

C:07

| What **are** you | | I'm | |
|---|---|---|---|
| What **are** they | doing? | They're | sleep**ing**. |
| What**'s** he/she | | He**'s**/She**'s** | |

**6** **Look at the scene. Circle.**

**1**  He's ( listening to music / doing homework ).

**2** She's ( dancing / cleaning ).

**3** She's ( eating / drinking ).

**4** They're ( walking / sleeping ).

**7** **Act, ask, and answer.**

What are you doing?

I'm reading.

**8**  **Listen and number. Then say.**

**a**  **b**  **c**  **d**  **e**

playing the piano | playing the trumpet | playing the flute | playing the violin | singing

**f**  **g**  **h**  **i**  **j**

**9**   **Listen and stick. Then sing.**

Are you ____ ? No, I'm not.

Are you singing? Yes, I am. I'm singing quietly. Can you hear me?

Are you ____ ? No, I'm not.

Are you playing the violin?

Yes, I am. I'm playing terribly.

Can you hear me?

Is she ____ ? No, she isn't.

Is she doing her homework?

Yes, she is. She's working quickly.

Wow! Now she's finished.

Is she ____ ? No, she isn't.

Is she dancing? Yes, she is. She's dancing slowly.

Wait! Now she's finished.

Can identify more activities and words that describe how you do them

**LOOK!**

C:11

| Are you singing? | Yes, I am. / No, I'm not. |
|---|---|
| Is he/she singing? | Yes, he/she is. / No, he/she isn't. |
| Is he/she singing quietly? | Yes, he/she is.<br>No, he/she isn't. He's/She's singing loudly. |

**10** C:12 **Listen and circle. Then ask and answer.**

1  Is he playing the piano quickly?   ( Yes, he is. / No, he isn't. )

2  Is she eating a cookie loudly?    ( Yes, she is. / No, she isn't. )

3  Is he drinking loudly?        ( Yes, he is. / No, he isn't. )

4  Is she dancing quickly?       ( Yes, she is. / No, she isn't. )

5  Is he singing terribly?       ( Yes, he is. / No, he isn't. )

> Is he playing the piano quickly?

> Yes, he is.

**11** C:13 **Listen and read. Then write.**

 **READING**

Dear Grandma and Grandpa,
We're at the beach. It's sunny and hot. I'm drinking juice and reading a book quietly. Tim's sleeping, and Dad's playing the violin. He's playing very loudly! Mom isn't here. She's running slowly on the beach. I can see her now. She's waving! We're all having fun! Please come next time.
Tracy

1  What is Tracy doing? She's _____ and reading.

2  Is Tim playing volleyball? No, _____. He's _____.

3  What is Dad doing? He's _____.

4  Is Mom running quickly on the beach? No, _____. She's _____.

  **Role-play the story.**

Can understand a simple story / Can role-play a story

**14** **Read and match the questions and answers about each picture.**

**Picture 1** Is Captain Conrad gardening?    **a** Yes, he does.

**Picture 2** Can PROD 2 see a tifftiff plant?    **b** No, he isn't.

**Picture 3** Does Captain Conrad have the tifftiff plant?    **c** They're running quickly.

**Picture 4** What are the tricksters doing?    **d** Yes, they are.

**Picture 5** Can the tricksters run now?    **e** Yes, he can.

**Picture 6** Are Kim and Katy happy?    **f** No, they can't.

**15**  **Write Y = Yes or N = No. Then ask and answer.**

**VALUES**

Learn new things. Develop your talents.

**1** Me ☐ My friend ☐
Sing.

**2** Me ☐ My friend ☐
Dance.

**3** Me ☐ My friend ☐
Act.

**4** Me ☐ My friend ☐
Paint.

**5** Me ☐ My friend ☐
Cook.

**6** Me ☐ My friend ☐
Play an instrument.

Can you sing?

Yes, I can.

**16**  **What do you know?**

**17**  **Listen and read. Then write _B_ = Balloon or _R_ = Rocket.**

## Flying machines

This is a hot-air balloon. It's very colorful. It doesn't have wings. It's flying on hot air. A pilot is flying the balloon very slowly. It's flying quietly above the clouds.

This isn't an airplane, it's a rocket. It's very big, and it can fly very quickly. There are three astronauts in this rocket. They're flying from Earth to space.

| | | |
|---|---|---|
| **1** | It's flying slowly above the clouds. | ☐ |
| **2** | It can fly quickly. | ☐ |
| **3** | It's flying on hot air. | ☐ |
| **4** | It's very colorful. | ☐ |
| **5** | It's flying to space. | ☐ |
| **6** | It's flying above the Earth. | ☐ |

Can understand short texts about flying machines

**18**   Make a flying machine. Talk to a friend.

1 **Think** about flying machines.
2 **Choose** and draw a flying machine.
3 **Make** a flying machine.
4 **Talk** about your flying machine.

**HOME SCHOOL LINK**

Show your flying machine to your family.

Look! It can fly!

**PHONICS**

**19**   **Listen.** C:16

① **left**  ② **bump**  ③ **wind**  ④ **paint**
⑤ **ask**  ⑥ **wisp**  ⑦ **nest**

**20**   **Listen and blend the sounds.** C:17

**21**  Underline *ft*, *mp*, *nd*, *nt*, *sk*, and *st*. Read the sentences aloud.

**1** I have a bump on my leg.

**2** The bird is in the nest.

**3** This is my left hand.

**4** Ask the artist to paint a cat.

**22** **Match. Then write a sentence.**

| 1 | eat | | **a** | to music | She _____. |
|---|-----|---|-------|----------|------|
| 2 | drink | | **b** | homework | They _____. |
| 3 | listen | | **c** | the tub | _____ you _____? |
| 4 | play | | **d** | juice | He _____. |
| 5 | read | | **e** | a book | _____ he _____? |
| 6 | do | | **f** | to school | They _____. |
| 7 | walk | | **g** | lunch | He's ____eating lunch____. |
| 8 | clean | | **h** | the trumpet | She _____. |

**23**  **Choose actions from Activity 22 and an adverb. Then ask and answer.**

| loudly | quickly | quietly | slowly | terribly |

Are you eating lunch quickly?

Yes, I am.

**24** **Draw a picture of you or a friend doing an action. Write.**

This is _____.

I'm/He's/She's _____.

**I CAN**

I can ask and answer about what people are doing.

I can talk about how people are doing activities.

I can understand short texts about flying machines.

**How many sentences can you make in five minutes? Look and write. Then say.**

cleaning  drinking  doing homework  eating  listening to music
playing basketball  playing the piano  playing the trumpet
reading  sleeping

I

He

She

They

They're listening to music in the living room.

She's sleeping in the bedroom.

**Now go to Poptropica English World**

**Lesson 10**

Can use what I have learned in Unit 8   **105**

# Review Units 7 and 8

**1** Circle the one that doesn't belong.

fish
meat
eggs
chicken
chocolate
pasta

cleaning
reading
amazing
drinking
eating
doing homework

**2** C:18 Listen and match.

Tracy ☐

Tim ☐

Can talk about food and actions

**Act, ask, and answer.**

**1**

**2**

**3**

**4**

**5**

**6**

What are you doing, Tim?

I'm sleeping.

# Goodbye

**1**  Listen, find, and number.

**2** Listen. Who is missing?

Can identify the story characters

**3**  **Listen and write. Then sing.**

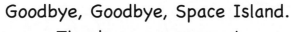

Goodbye, Goodbye, Space Island.
Thank you, everyone!
We like the park, the ¹_____, the sports center, the café,
Fid's house, the fruits, the flowers, the ²_____.
But most of all, we like the tifftiff plant!
Hooray! Hooray! Hooray!

Now Katy, Kim, and the captain are ³_____ home to Earth.
Say goodbye to PROD 1 and 2. Say ⁴_____ one more time.
Goodbye, Katy. Goodbye, Kim.
See you again another day!

**4**  **Ask and answer.**

My favorite character is...

My favorite story is about...

My favorite song is about...

**1** Who's your favorite character?

**2** What's your favorite song about?

**3** What's your favorite story about?

**5** **Draw or stick pictures. Then write.**

My favorite nature scene

There is _____.

There are _____

_____.

There aren't any _____.

My pet

My pet is a _____.

It has _____.

It doesn't have _____.

It is so _____.

I love my pet.

**6** **Draw or stick a picture of you in your home. Then write.**

This is me in my _____

_____ (room).

I have _____ hair

and _____ eyes.

I'm wearing _____

and _____. These are

my favorite clothes.

My _____ (room) is great.

There is _____.

There are _____.

Can write about what I have learned

**7** **Draw or stick pictures of what you can or can't do. Then write.**

I can _____

_____ .

I can _____

_____ .

I can't _____

_____ .

**8** **Draw or stick pictures of your family. Then write.**

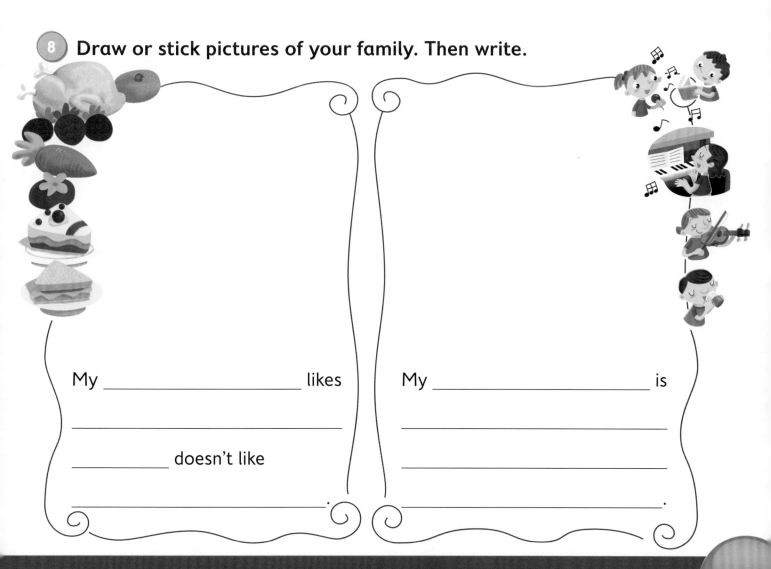

My _____ likes

_____

_____ doesn't like

_____ .

My _____ is

_____

_____

_____ .

# Halloween

**1** 🎧 C:23 Listen, find, and say.

ghost

witch

broom

spider

pumpkin

hat

Can sing a song about Halloween

bat

Trick or treat,
Trick or treat,
Give us something good to eat.
Give us candy,
Give us cupcakes,
Give us something good to take.
If you don't,
Hee, hee, hee,
We'll put spiders in your tea!

Trick or treat,
Trick or treat,
Give us something good to eat.
Give us cookies,
Give us cupcakes,
Give us something good to take.
If you don't,
Ha, ha, ha,
We'll put bats in your hat!

3 **Look and answer.**

1    How many pumpkins are there?

2    How many ghosts are there?

3    How many witches are there?

4    How many brooms are there?

5    How many bats are there?

6    How many hats are there?

7    How many spiders are there?

# April Fools' Day

**1**  **Read. Then listen and say.**

April Fools' Day is the first day of April. On April Fools' Day, people play jokes on their friends.

fool

fun

surprise

joke

**2**  **Listen and sing.**

It's the first day of April,
April Fools' Day.
It's the first day of April,
Surprise your friends, hooray!

... Fun and jokes, hooray!
... Fool your friends, hooray!
... I love this funny day!

**3** **Read the jokes and find the answer.**

| **1** What do sea monsters have for lunch? | **2** What's a rabbit's favorite music? | **3** What do you call a bear without an ear? |
|---|---|---|
| **a** Hip-hop | **b** B | **c** Fish and ships |

Can sing a song about April Fools' Day

# Earth Day

**1** **Read.**

Earth Day is April 22nd every year. It's a day to think about our planet and protect the environment.

**2** **Listen and point.** C:27

**a**

Plant a tree.

**b**

Turn off the lights.

**c**

Recycle.

**d**

Ride your bike.

**3** **Ask and answer.**

Yes, I do.

Do you turn off the lights?

**Earth Day**

# Wordlist

**Acknowledgments**

The Publishers would like to thank the following teachers for their suggestions and comments on this course:

Nurhan Deniz, Alejandra Juarez, Lara Ozer, Cynthia Xu, Basia Zarzycka

Jennifer Dobson, Anabel Higuera Gonzalez, Honorata Klosak, Dr Marianne Nikolov, Regina Ramalho

Asako Abe, JiEun Ahn, Nubia Isabel Albarracín, José Antonio Aranda Fuentes, Juritza Ardila, María del Carmen Ávila Tapia, Ernestina Baena, Marisela Bautista, Carmen Bautista, Norma Verónica Blanco, Suzette Bradford, Rose Brisbane, María Ernestina Bueno Rodríguez, María del Rosario Camargo Gómez, Maira Cantillo, Betsabé Cárdenas, María Cristina Castañeda, Carol Chen, Carrie Chen, Alice Chio, Tina Cho, Vicky Chung, Marcela Correa, Rosalinda Ponce de Leon, Betty Deng, Rhiannon Doherty, Esther Domínguez, Elizabeth Domínguez, Ren Dongmei, Gerardo Fernández, Catherine Gillis, Lois Gu, SoRa Han, Michelle He, María del Carmen Hernández, Suh Heui, Ryan Hillstead, JoJo Hong, Cindy Huang, Mie Inoue, Chiami Inoue, SoYun Jeong, Verónica Jiménez, Qi Jing, Sunshui Jing, Maiko Kainuma, YoungJin Kang, Chisato Kariya, Yoko Kato, Eriko Kawada, Sanae Kawamoto, Sarah Ker, Sheely Ker, Hyomin Kim, Lee Knight, Akiyo Kumazawa, JinJu Lee, Eunchae Lee, Jin-Yi Lee, Sharlene Liao, Yu Ya Link, Marcela Maruchi, Hilda Martínez Rosal, Alejandro Mateos Chávez, Cristina Medina Gómez, Bertha Elsi Méndez, Luz del Carmen Mercado, Ana Morales, Ana Estela Morales, Zita Morales Cruz, Shinano Murata, Junko Nishikawa, Sawako Ogawa, Ikuko Okada, Hiroko Okuno, Tomomi Owaki, Sayil Palacio Trejo, Rosa Lilia Paniagua, MiSook Park, SeonJeong Park, JoonYong Park, María Eugenia Pastrana, Silvia Santana Paulino, Dulce María Pineda, Rosalinda Ponce de León, Liliana Porras, María Elena Portugal, Yazmín Reyes, Diana Rivas Aguilar, Rosa Rivera Espinoza, Nayelli Guadalupe Rivera Martínez, Araceli Rivero Martínez, David Robin, Angélica Rodríguez, Leticia Santacruz Rodríguez, Silvia Santana Paulino, Kate Sato, Cassie Savoie, Mark Savoie, Yuki Scott, Yoshiko Shimoto, Jeehye Shin, MiYoung Song, Lisa Styles, Laura Sutton, Mayumi Tabuchi, Takako Takagi, Miriam Talonia, Yoshiko Tanaka, María Isabel Tenorio, Chioko Terui, José Francisco Trenado, Yasuko Tsujimoto, Elmer Usaguen, Hiroko Usami, Michael Valentine, José Javier Vargas, Nubia Margot Vargas, Guadalupe Vázquez, Norma Velázquez Gutiérrez, Ruth Marina Venegas, María Martha Villegas Rodríguez, Heidi Wang, Tomiko Watanabe, Jamie Wells, Susan Wu, Junko Yamaguchi, Dai Yang, Judy Yao, Yo Yo, Sally Yu, Mary Zhou, Rose Zhuang

# Stickers

## Unit 2 **Me** page 30

## Unit 3 **Pets** page 42

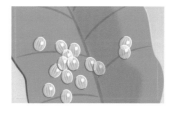

## Unit 4 **Home** page 51

## Unit 6 **Sports** page 75

# Unit 5 **Clothes** page 69

# Unit 7 **Food** page 87

# Unit 8 **Things we do** page 98